SPEAKING
FOR ISRAEL

A Speechwriter Battles Anti-Israel
Opinions at the United Nations

AVIVA KLOMPAS
PREFACE BY ALAN DERSHOWITZ

Skyhorse Publishing

For my parents,
my first editors and lasting champions.

Skyhorse Publishing books may be purchased in bulk at special discounts for sales promotion, corporate gifts, fund-raising, or educational purposes. Special editions can also be created to specifications. For details, contact the Special Sales Department, Skyhorse Publishing, 307 West 36th Street, 11th Floor, New York, NY 10018 or info@skyhorsepublishing.com.

Skyhorse® and Skyhorse Publishing® are registered trademarks of Skyhorse Publishing, Inc.®, a Delaware corporation.

Visit our website at www.skyhorsepublishing.com.

10 9 8 7 6 5 4 3 2 1

Library of Congress Cataloging-in-Publication Data is available on file.

Cover design by Paul Qualcom

Print ISBN: 978-1-5107-4391-5
Ebook ISBN: 978-1-5107-4392-2

Printed in the United States of America

Contents

Preface

By Alan Dershowitz

Every year the United Nations Human Rights Council convenes a conference to consider the issues of human rights and human wrongs around the world. But like the United Nations itself, the focus on alleged human wrongs is always on the one democracy in the middle east, namely Israel. Despite the fact that no country in the world faced with threats comparable to those faced by Israel has a better human rights record, the United Nations and its agencies condemn Israel more than all the other countries in the world combined.

In 2009, the Human Rights Council convened in Geneva. The principle speaker on Human rights was Mahmoud Ahmadinejad, who at the time was ordering the murder of gays, heretics and dissidents, and sponsoring terrorism around the world. I was there, with others, protesting. Then, in 2010 when the Human Rights Council convened in New York, I gave a speech in front of the United Nations which included the following criticisms:

One important reason why there is no peace in the Middle East can be summarized tragically in two letters, UN. The building dedicated in theory to pace has facilitated terrorism, stood idly by genocide, given a platform to Holocaust deniers, and disincentivized the Palestinians from negotiating a two-state solution . . . How dare states such as Saudi Arabia, Cuba, Venezuela, Zimbabwe, Iran, Bahrain, Syria, Belarus and other tyrannies too numerous to mention lecture Israel about human rights? How dare states such as Turkey, that have attacked their own Kurdish minorities and Armenian minorities, and Russia, which has attacked its own Chechnyan minority . . . lecture Israel about Peace?

Is there no sense of shame . . . ? Has the word hypocrisy lost its meaning . . . ? Does no one recognize the need for a single neutral standard of human rights? Have human rights now become the permanent weapon of choice for those who practice human wrongs. For shame. For shame.

When I engaged in these protests, I wish I had had with me the book *Speaking for Israel* by Aviva Klompas, who for years wrote speeches and spoke articulately about the bias of the United Nations in general and the Human Rights Council in particular against the nation state of the Jewish people. Her book illuminates how the United Nations, the very institution which in 1947 voted to partition the British Mandate into two states for two peoples, has grievously set back the cause of human rights and promoted human wrongs.

Oh how things have changed over the past seventy-two years since the global body's founding. Can they ever change back? To answer that question, please read this book and ponder its wise words.

—Alan Dershowitz
Author, *Defending Israel: The Story of My Relationship
with My Most Challenging Client*

Author's Note

This book is based on the time I spent working as the speechwriter in the Permanent Mission of Israel to the United Nations. Many names have been changed, I have taken certain liberties with the chronology and dialogue, and, with the passage of time, some circumstances are undoubtedly imperfectly remembered. I wrote this book to share a remarkable time in my life. I feel privileged to have worked alongside so many extraordinary people and am profoundly grateful for the experience. Write on.

Introduction

If I ever have the chance to meet Aaron Sorkin, I will thank him profusely. His immensely popular and critically acclaimed television series, *The West Wing*, seems to be responsible for the fascination and admiration surrounding speechwriters. Thanks to his show, when people learn I was the speechwriter for Israel's ambassador to the United Nations, they conjure images of days spent fighting on the side of the angels, armed with witty banter and righteous certainty developed from years studying the Middle East.

That's not my story. I grew up in Toronto, majored in zoology, and spent my early career working on domestic provincial policy issues. The diplomats and staff of Israel's delegation to the United Nations weren't angels. Far from it. We were people with egos and eccentricities, ambitions and attitude, fears and failings. But we shared a common purpose.

In my first week of work, one of the diplomats came bounding into my office, and in the abrupt manner of an Israeli, asked me why I would leave a calm and comfortable job in Canada to work around the clock for one of the most unpopular countries in the world. She ended her question by saying, "*hishtagat?*" which is Hebrew for, "*Are you crazy?*"

Before she came in, I had been staring dejectedly at the jam-packed speech schedule and her question did nothing to raise my spirits. It was only a few days into my new position, but I could see that working with Israelis was going to be an adjustment. My new colleagues were loud, stubborn, demanding, and had an unnerving habit of saying exactly what was on their minds.

Even so, it was a fair question. We were not shortlisted to win any popularity contests in the global body. Representing Israel at the United Nations is like volunteering to sell Boston Red Sox paraphernalia outside Yankee Stadium. It would have been bad enough to be silently scorned, but Israel, with just 0.1 percent of the world's population and 0.004 percent of the planetary landmass, consumes an overwhelming proportion of the global body's criticisms. My colleagues couldn't fathom why a non-Israeli would be willing to endure the stress and struggles of representing Israel in an institution notorious for its bias against the Jewish state.

The answer is that I believe Israel is more than just a country. I see it as a living testament to a small people's ability to overcome impossible odds through the sheer force of their commitment to knowledge, freedom, and innovation. I was immensely proud to go to work each day to represent the Jewish state in one of the world's most anti-Israel institutions. It was a remarkable time to be representing Israel on the global stage. During my tenure, I saw the collapse of four Middle Eastern states, faltering Israeli-Palestinian peace talks, waves of Palestinian terrorism, stop-and-go nuclear negotiations culminating in the Iran deal, an attempt to push Palestinian statehood through the Security Council, the Palestinians' bid to join the International Criminal Court, the kidnapping and murder of three Israeli teenagers—Eyal, Gilad, and Naftali—and fifty days of war between Israel and Hamas in Gaza.

This book tells the story of how an aspiring evolutionary biologist from Canada became an author of Israel's voice on the world stage of the United Nations.

CHAPTER 1

Yalla! / Let's go!

What do you say when you can't say no?

I had been working in the Israeli delegation to the United Nations for a few months when I was contacted by a lecturer at the New School in New York City and asked to give a presentation to her class on how to become a speechwriter. I cheerfully accepted, hung up the phone, then promptly went to find my interns and asked them to research how one becomes a speechwriter. It sounds ridiculous, but I could hardly stand up in front of a class of students and encourage them to follow in my footsteps—study zoology in university, became a policy advisor in Canada, and then hope to get a call out of the blue from the Israeli government.

Growing up, I was not a talented writer. My parents are quick to point this out to anyone who asks if they recognized any early prodigious skills. "Certainly not in the school papers we had to mark up in red ink," they share a little too eagerly. Uncertain of the career I wanted to pursue after high school, I enrolled in the University of Toronto's science program. Fascinated by a first-year course on evolutionary behavior, I decided to major in zoology and minor in eighteenth-century Enlightenment history. My parents had concerns.

By my final year of college, it was clear I wasn't going to follow in the footsteps of Darwin or Herodotus, and my unusual combination of courses wasn't setting me up for steady income after graduation. My mother, a high school career counselor, wordlessly left printouts of various post-college programs with a more practical bent for me to happen upon. One caught my interest, and I enrolled in a postgraduate corporate communications program. Freed from the burden of writing long, dense academic papers, I happily discovered I was a decent writer. I decided to combine my interest in the sciences and communications and applied for a policy and communications position in a healthcare association. In the interview, Andrew, my prospective boss, asked what I believed to be my greatest weakness. Surprised by the question and unprepared with rehearsed answers like "I'm a workaholic" or "I'm a perfectionist," I told him the truth, "My writing could be better."

He later told me he could not believe that while interviewing for a communications job, I admitted I needed to work on my writing skills. Apparently, my obliviousness was endearing, and Andrew felt he could coach me, because he offered me the position. The job came with a promise that he and his communications team would turn me into a first-class writer. They taught me that good writing is right, tight, and bright, and set me to work drafting everything from policy briefing notes to newspaper articles to speeches for the CEO. I loved my job and adored my colleagues. Our little team encouraged good-natured fun, especially in the form of pranks. For an annual fundraiser, we held an auction of challenges for colleagues. I wagered enough to see a coworker, whose politics ran slightly to the right of the Kremlin, walk up and down Toronto's bustling Front Street, wearing a sandwich board encouraging cars to honk if they loved the local liberal radio station.

I eventually left my position in the healthcare association to begin work on a master's degree in public policy at New York University's Wagner School. This time around, I was intent on getting practical experience that could lead to a paying job after graduation. Step one was landing an internship in the Office of the Public Advocate for the City of New York, working on environment and education issues. The following semester, I interned at the United Nations Development Fund for Women (UNIFEM), garnering support for the global campaign to end violence against women.

My final year of school included a capstone project in which students worked in small consulting teams to address a pressing social question. My team worked with a nonprofit that creates economic opportunity for unemployed youth in the Middle East and North Africa by providing training to improve their economic future and that of their countries. Our project sent us to Jordan and Morocco to test a monitoring and evaluation framework for their students and staff.

Bitten by the travel bug, I also volunteered to lead Birthright. The free ten-day trip offers young Jewish adults the chance to tour Israel. Staffing these trips was immensely rewarding, and when I returned to New York, I sent an effusive email to friends and family describing my experience. I wrote that I would love to sit with the founding philanthropists to hear their impressions on the program. A few days later, I got a phone call inviting me to meet Charles Bronfman, one of the founders of the Birthright program. My friend Tali had shared my email with her father, who in turn, shared it with Bronfman's office. On the appointed day, I arrived at Mr. Bronfman's office and looked around in awe at the beautifully adorned space.

We chatted for a while, until Mr. Bronfman abruptly said, "You should meet Asi." I nodded in agreement, having no idea who Asi was or why I should meet with him. A couple of weeks later, I got a call from the Consulate of Israel in New York inviting me to meet "Asi"—who turned out to be Israel's consul general in New York City. I arrived in his office, and after some initial pleasantries, the consul general asked me why Bronfman felt I should meet with him. Having no idea, I told him as much which led to an awkward silence. Deciding Bronfman must have sent me his way for a reason, he asked about school and my career aspirations and if I was interested in interning at the Consulate. At the time, I was interning at UNIFEM and was perfectly happy with my position. Seeing I was about to turn him down and adeptly sidestepping another awkward silence he said, "Think about it. You can start next semester."

I ended up interning at the Israeli Consulate, doing the many tedious things interns do: data entry, phone calls, photocopying, and the like. From time to time, I was asked to help write speeches for the consul general. I would draft remarks and then sit with his Israeli speechwriter and pore over every sentence.

"It don't—eh—sound good," he would insist, and continue, "Are you sure, it shouldn't—eh—be with the words backwards?"

I would patiently try to explain English grammar, but it was a losing battle because he would ultimately write what he thought "sounded good."

As spring approached, I decided that after graduation I wanted to enter the field of public policy back home in Canada, and so applied for a slew of government positions. My last semester flew by and suddenly graduation arrived in a spectacular display of purple-clad NYU gowns flocking around Washington Square Park. A few days later, I packed up my New York apartment and moved home to Toronto to take a position in the Ontario government.

I held several policy positions in government, but the bulk of my time was spent working for Deputy Minister Jim Stephens. Kind, charismatic, well read, and well rounded, Jim was the sort of principled leader I hoped to work for. He had left a successful career in the private sector and moved to government to make a difference. Jim enjoyed public speaking but wasn't happy with the speeches being written for him out of the ministry's Communications Division. I offered to step in for a couple remarks and before long, I was both his policy advisor and primary speechwriter. The best thing about writing for Jim was that he was interested in everything. Most of his speeches focused on leadership and the need to modernize government; he gave me free reign to use whatever factoids and stories I wanted to inspire people to be a part of the progressive, proud, and responsible civil service he envisioned. The speeches I wrote ran the gamut—I told the story behind the mega success of the Starbucks coffee chain, explained how we can learn moral courage from baseball players, and even wrote a speech on the periodic table of elements. I loved writing creative speeches and Jim loved delivering them.

Eventually, I left Jim's office to join the Cabinet Office and oversee the portfolios of the ministries of Transportation and Infrastructure. Six months into the job, I took a vacation to lead my tenth Birthright group. My group was scheduled to depart from New York City, and I arrived in the city a couple days early to spend time with friends. I met my friend Tali for dinner; we caught up on things and talked about our jobs. She was working for Israel's economic mission and had heard about an open position in the Israeli Mission to the United Nations. She asked if I would be interested in working for the Israeli government, and I laughed off the question saying, "Sure, why not?"

The next day as I was walking along Thirty-Fourth Street in Manhattan, my phone rang. It was loud on the street, and, expecting it was my mother checking in, I answered saying, "I'll just step into Victoria's Secret so I can hear you." The person on the phone paused momentarily before launching into a rapid outburst and shooting off questions without waiting for answers. It was most definitely not my mother. The distinctly male voice continued, undeterred by my silence. Eventually, I interrupted and said, "I'm sorry, but who is this?"

The person on the other end of the line let out an impatient sigh and then said, "My name is Nate Miller and I'm the speechwriter for Israel's ambassador to the UN." Confused, I listened as he continued, "You're a speechwriter, correct?"

"Well yes, no, sort of." Ignoring my ineloquence, Nate steamed ahead.

"You've written speeches?" he demanded.

"Yes," I answered unsurely.

"Great, send me a few."

I tried to explain I was on vacation and on my way to Israel and didn't have my computer or access to my files.

"You'll figure it out. I'm sending you an email. Reply to the email with the writing samples." He ordered before he abruptly hung up. I stepped out of Victoria's Secret and stood blinking in the winter sunshine.

There was no way I was going to upend my life by moving back to New York, I thought. I made my way along Thirty-Fourth Street for a few blocks and found myself in front of CUNY, where my childhood best friend, Naomi, worked. I went up to her office and relayed the phone call. Ever pragmatic, she pointed to the computer on her desk and said, "Search your email for some speeches and send them to him."

I searched through my email and discovered three old speeches I had written for Jim. Tapping out a quick note, I sent the speeches to Nate, sat back, and waited. Fifteen minutes later, I got a reply: *Send your passport information. You'll come meet the ambassador tomorrow.*

I stared at the screen for a while and then turned to Naomi to read Nate's response aloud.

"I have a flight to Israel tomorrow and I'm not looking for a new job."

"Just go and hear what he has to say." Naomi urged.

"I can't. I didn't pack any 'meet the ambassador' clothes," I griped.

Naomi wheeled her chair toward me, stared hard at me, and said, "This isn't really up to you." She continued, "If you don't get the job, you have a great story to tell about the time you were interviewed by an ambassador. But, if you are offered the job, there is no real choice—this is a job you don't turn down."

I let her words sink in, then said, "Israel is a very casual country. People get married in khakis and short sleeved shirts. I can probably go meet the ambassador in jeans, right?"

Naomi sighed, handed me my coat, and said, "There's a Banana Republic down the street."

An hour later I walked out of the store with a dress slung over my arm, and made my way toward my hotel to read up on Israel's sixteenth ambassador to the United Nations.

Ambassador Ron Prosor was born in Kfar Saba in 1958, ten years after the establishment of the State of Israel. He joined the Foreign Ministry in 1986 and was appointed to increasingly senior positions. He was one of the first Israeli representatives to establish ties with East Germany, later became a political advisor to the Israeli Embassy in Washington, participated in negotiations prior to the signing of the Wye Agreement, and was a member of the Camp David delegation. He served as director-general of the Foreign Ministry during the controversial withdrawal from the Gaza Strip in 2005, became Israel's ambassador to the United Kingdom from 2007 to 2011, and then landed the role as Israel's permanent representative to the United Nations in 2011.

One of Israel's highest profile advocates, Ron made a name for himself speaking candidly and colorfully in defense of the Jewish state, using sarcasm and humor to garner attention. He is forthright, charming, articulate, and has a penchant for liberally sprinkling his remarks with puns, rhetorical questions, and cynical retorts.

The following day, at the appointed time, I stood across the street from the imposing building on Second Avenue that houses the Israeli Mission to the United Nations. Looking up, I saw an Israeli flag fluttering from a low roof on the side of the building. Shoulders fixed, I crossed the street, pulled open the heavy doors, and found myself face to face with a young man in a suit, earpiece clearly visible. With a distinctly Israeli accent, he asked, "Can I help you?"

After navigating security, I was escorted upstairs and instructed to sit in a small makeshift waiting area just outside the ambassador's office. I took a seat and was about to lean over to pick up a brochure when Nate arrived and introduced himself. He was tall, sporting trendy eye glasses, with a mop of unruly hair that bounced as he walked. Nate sat down beside me, and we discussed details of the position. He had a habit of nodding his head rapidly as he listened and then answering in rapid-fire staccato. I immediately liked him.

Eventually I was called into the ambassador's office. Nate escorted me into the room and we were followed by two stylishly dressed women, both of whom exuded an aura of no nonsense. The first, Dafna, was deeply tanned, with highlighted hair and a manner that suggested she had no time to waste. The second, Ella, was a larger woman with short, sleek dark hair and a slight gap between her two front teeth. They ushered me into Ron's office. I sat down on a leather couch and gazed around the room. At the far end was a large desk and adjoining table that held a computer. A flat screen television was affixed to the wall above, and an Israeli flag was positioned nearby. The desk was covered in neat stacks of paper and an assortment of plaques.

Ron gestured for me to sit in one of the armchairs facing a brown leather sofa. Between us was a wooden coffee table with a simple decorative border. Running the expanse of one wall were dark wood bookcases jammed with books, ornaments, and framed photographs. I could make out photos of Ron with Benjamin Netanyahu, Shimon Peres, Barack and Michelle Obama, Bill Clinton, Queen Elizabeth, and Pope John Paul II.

The wall by the door was adorned with photos of Ron with Sharon Stone, Angelina Jolie, and Richard Gere. There was also a single large framed photograph that I later learned held a special place in Ron's heart. It had hung in his various offices for over two decades and was often the first thing he showed visitors. Photographed in Cairo in 1994, Ron calls it "the Middle East without Words." In the photo, Yitzhak Rabin stands to the side, arms folded in a clear expression of fury. Nearby, then foreign minister Shimon Peres points his finger angrily in Yasser Arafat's face. Arafat stands alongside Russian foreign minister Andrey Kozyrev, King Hussein of Jordan, US secretary of state Warren Christopher, and President Hosni Mubarak of Egypt. Ron delighted in telling his visitors that seconds earlier, Mubarak had called Arafat a son of a dog in Arabic.

Ron came around his desk and stood across from me. He was only a little taller than me but walked with an air of authority that seemed to add feet to his stature. We shook hands before he unbuttoned his pressed suit jacket and sank into one of the leather armchairs. Crossing one leg over the other, his highly-shined shoe bounced slightly as he surveyed me. I, in turn, took in his solid build, round face, sharp eyes, graying beard, and shiny bald head. In English tinged with British and Israeli accents, Ron asked where I grew up and went to school, about my previous jobs, and what I thought of his speeches.

He listened to my answers and then explained that his speechwriter was also expected to write op-eds. Staring at me intently, he asked me to pitch an idea for an article. The question took me by surprise and as I saw four sets of eyes gazing intently at me, I drew a blank. I had recently heard an Israeli rocket scientist give a presentation on Iron Dome, Israel's famed mobile missile defense system. During Operation Pillar of Defense, a couple of months earlier in November 2012, it had successfully protected Israeli citizens from the barrage of rockets launched by Hamas terrorists in Gaza. I suggested an op-ed describing how the hero of Israel's military operations was a self-defense system rather than an offensive system.

I had barely finished my sentence, before Ron said, "That would have been a good idea during the operation, but what have you got that can run this week?"

I wracked my brain and finally answered, "Ron, I'm not sure if your staff told you that I came to New York for two days of vacation before leading a Birthright trip. I never imagined I'd be attending an interview and I have to confess that I am not properly prepared."

The room went silent.

Ron regarded me a while longer before he turned to Nate and said, "Take her to a computer and have her write an op-ed."

With that, he stood, and I was summarily dismissed.

Nate led me down the hall. I glanced at my watch and said, "Nate, I only have half an hour before I have to leave to make my flight."

"Don't worry about it," he replied.

Nate led me down the corridor into a narrow room lined with two rows of desks and computers facing the wall. Pointing to one of the computers he said, "Write about the situation in Mali." He turned to an impossibly tall guy in a kippa (a yarmulke) standing nearby and said, "She doesn't have security clearance so watch her." He glanced over and nodded at me.

I later discovered this was Avishai, Nate's intern. When I eventually joined the Mission, Avishai and I became close friends. In fact, my first few months at the Mission were made tolerable by his kindness, patient guidance, and tremendous writing talent.

I slowly sat down at the computer and racked my brain to recall what I had read earlier about Mali. I could recount vague details of France threatening to bomb targets in Mali where Islamist rebels had established a stronghold. I turned to my tall sentry and asked if I could search the web. He nodded and turned to his own work on a nearby computer.

I scrolled through news sites and began writing an article on the need for Western nations to take the fight to the terrorists to prevent them from advancing any closer to Europe. With barely thirty minutes to write something, I typed as quickly as I could, using brackets for placeholder thoughts such as [insert description of why terrorism is a scourge on all peoples]. I think I managed to get four hundred words written before I reluctantly stood and explained that I had to get to the airport to meet my Birthright group.

A year later, Ron and I had lunch together and reminisced about my bizarre interview. He told me he knew he would offer me the job when, "Faced with an impossible task—writing an op-ed in half an hour, you didn't say it was unrealistic and you didn't make excuses, you sat down and got to work."

I didn't understand this at the time of my interview, but there is a specific mindset needed to work for a nation constantly under attack diplomatically, economically, legally, and militarily. You can't be easily deterred or succumb to situations that seem unfair or impossible. You need a certain courage of conviction to deflect the constant attacks. Israel's first prime minister, David Ben-Gurion, wisely said, "The difficult we do immediately, the impossible takes a little longer." That's the attitude needed to successfully represent Israel in an institution where many delegates harbor anti-Semitic views, question the right of your people to have a state of their own, or pay no mind to those who seek to wipe you off the face of the earth.

Nate reappeared and escorted me to the elevators. As we waited for the doors to open, he said, "I think you're the right person for this job. You need to think seriously about what you will say if it is offered to you."

My time interning for the Israeli Consulate during graduate school had taught me that Israel's Foreign Ministry pays horribly. As I stepped into the elevator, I asked Nate what the job paid. Even expecting the worst, I was shocked by the paltry figure. My heart sank as the doors closed. Nate yelled, "We'll talk!"

As I sat in the taxi weaving its way toward JFK airport, I was lost in thought. I had already done a stint living in New York and was happy in Toronto. I had a great government job with excellent prospects, an amazing apartment with a fifteen-foot balcony, and my beloved purple PT Cruiser. I was comfortable. And yet . . .

It was ridiculous to obsess over a job I hadn't even been offered yet, so I pushed the thought from my mind. At the airport, I found my Birthright group and turned my mind to enjoying our time in Israel. It was a struggle because every other day I would get a phone call from the Israeli Mission. Someone with an Israeli accent would instruct, "You have passed another phase of negotiations—but to be clear, we have not offered you the job." The rest of these conversations played out in a similar fashion. I would bemoan the fact that the salary was impossibly low, the benefits almost nonexistent, that moving expenses were not covered, and the fact that they had no intention of providing me with a cell phone despite the expectation to be on call 24/7. In every conversation, I righteously declared the expectations unreasonable and the parameters outrageous.

But Naomi's words rang through my head, "This is a job you don't turn down." On my last evening in Israel, Dafna, the ambassador's closest advisor, called to tell me I had progressed through all the rounds and they were formally offering me the job. I was sitting in a small café on Jerusalem's trendy Emek Refaim street having dinner with a friend. They hadn't agreed to a single one of my hiring requests, but I accepted the offer on the spot.

In early February, I flew from Israel to Toronto, gave notice at work, and set to work packing up my apartment. A few days later, I got an email from the Israeli Mission asking to arrange a meeting via Skype so I could meet the deputy ambassador. He had been on vacation when I visited the mission and was understandably curious about who had been hired as the new speechwriter.

When the interview began, I discovered that my head was filling a massive television screen in a nondescript boardroom. Around a large boardroom table sat half a dozen individuals who were not introduced to me. The deputy ambassador began by asking about my current work as a speechwriter. I replied, "I'm actually not a speechwriter at the moment, I'm a government policy advisor . . . but I am a senior advisor."

He stared at me a moment, before continuing, "But you're working on Middle Eastern policy, right?"

"Not exactly. Actually, no, not at all. I work on provincial transportation and infrastructure policy."

"But you used to work in Middle Eastern diplomacy?"

"Not *per se* . . . ." I trailed off.

"You have a degree in international relations?"

"Zoology actually."

I could see the wheels in his head turning as he struggled to understand if this was some sort of elaborate joke. It was a thought we likely shared many times in the coming months.

In addition to wrapping up my affairs in Toronto, I began the lengthy security clearance process. I had been through a security process before beginning my internship at the Israeli Consulate and was somewhat prepared for the myriad questions and the long wait that followed. Late in March, I got a call telling me I had cleared security and could begin working at the Mission.

My first day of work was April 15, 2013. It also happened to be Yom Hazikaron, Israel's Remembrance Day for soldiers and victims of terror attacks. It was a poignant start to my new position. Around midday, we heard reports that two bombs had gone off near the finish line of the Boston Marathon, killing three spectators and wounding more than 260 people. That evening, the Israeli Mission was hosting a Yom Ha'atzmaut reception at the United Nations to celebrate Israel's Independence Day. I arrived at the tent set up overlooking the East River and made a beeline for Ella, Ron's chief of staff. The ambassador was planning to deliver brief remarks at the reception. I asked if he should refer to the Boston attack. Ella told me she'd already called Ron and they simply wanted to pay tribute to the victims of the attack without drawing any comparisons to terror in Israel. Nodding, I pulled out a piece of paper from my bag and began scribbling additional lines for Ron's speech. He would express his condolences to the victims, their families, and the citizens of Boston and then continue with his prepared remarks. When Ron arrived, he looked at the new lines, nodded, and tucked the paper into his suit pocket. My job done, I headed for the bar to get a drink and found Avishai. We listened to Ron deliver his remarks and when he was done, partook in the three pillars of diplomacy—protocol, cholesterol, and alcohol.

CHAPTER 2

Hishtagat? / Are you crazy?

What rank do I need to declare war?

The first hour of my first day of work began in the Mission's Human Resources department. I sat at a small table in the middle of the department for an orientation session. In the rote manner of someone who had given the same speech hundreds of time, a woman from HR ticked her way through a list.

Work hours: "You sign in and out every day using fingerprint scanning, if you come in late or leave early, we deduct your pay."

Vacation: "You must fill out a form and have it signed by a supervisor and submitted to us before taking vacation. The form must say where you are going, how you can be reached, and who will be covering your duties at work. If you take more vacation days than you are allotted, we deduct your pay."

Sick days: "You are entitled to a limited number of sick days. If you are away two days in a row, you need to bring us a doctor's note. If you are sick more than twice, we want a doctor's note every time you call in sick going forward. No note, no pay."

Overtime: "You are entitled to overtime pay, but security requires you to leave the building by a certain time every evening. You cannot come to the office earlier than security permits and you cannot come into the building on weekends or holidays. You will often have to work from home. We don't pay you for hours worked outside of the office."

I listened as she detailed an HR system that seemed to be designed to avoid paying its employees. I would soon discover that while HR considered a work day to consist of seven hours, it was common for me to work twelve hours a day, and longer if I attended evening or weekend events. Not long after I started, HR sent me a letter stipulating my paid overtime hours would be capped at twenty-five hours per week. It was so absurd that I laughed out loud. Twenty-five hours was roughly the number of overtime hours I worked on a busy weekend.

Periodically, I would receive perplexing letters from HR. Three months into the job, I was sent a letter informing me I had been promoted to rank 108. I was delighted. Until that point I had no idea that I even had a rank. I reread my letter and wondered with delight what rank the prime minister held. Supposing he was rank 1, I was just 107 promotions away from the country's top job. The Israeli Parliament has 120 members and I enjoyed imagining there were at least a dozen members that I—a Canadian—already outranked. I shared my theory with a colleague and, as was often the case, was met with a blank stare.

But I digress. Having finally exhausted the orientation checklist in front of her, the HR coordinator escorted us upstairs and dropped me off with Avishai. He seemed even taller than when I had met him during my interview. I followed as he led me around the corridor to a narrow room with two desks and three doorways. Pointing to the door on the far left, he said, "That's your office." Standing in the doorway, I surveyed the dark and grungy room.

Two of the overhead lights were burnt out and the walls were scuffed and pockmarked. A whiteboard hung on the wall with remnants of someone's old to-do list. Business cards, paperclips, and napkins littered the top of the desk. Papers, broken umbrellas, dated UN handbooks, binders, and knick-knacks were crammed into the shelves along with stacks of books.

Cheerfully, Avishai told me, "Cleanliness wasn't Nate's priority, but we got rid of the worst of the junk." He didn't seem to be kidding.

"Anyway," he said, as he kicked aside some papers that had fallen from the shelf, "I'm working on a social media post, so I'll let you settle in and come see you later." With that he turned and left me alone in my new office.

Gingerly I eased myself into the large black chair and surveyed my desk. The monitor was splattered with something and the keyboard crunched as I tentatively pressed down on the keys. Cautiously, I opened the desk drawers and found them filled with wadded notes, more old business cards, and crumbs.

I retrieved a roll of paper towels and a couple of garbage bags from the kitchen and set to work. The maintenance staff dropped off a stack of boxes with instructions to fill them with any papers and binders I wanted cleared away. I got to work pulling old binders and files from the shelf. Flipping through, I discovered a treasure trove of typewritten speeches, including a few delivered by Benjamin Netanyahu when he served as Israel's ambassador to the United Nation in the 1980s. It seemed the office hadn't been cleaned since then. I organized the old speeches into binders and returned them to the shelf, then filled the boxes with stacks of outdated reports, brochures, and magazines.

Hours later, I settled into my black desk chair and reviewed the list of upcoming speeches. Avishai showed me the calendar of upcoming events and explained what would be needed. That evening would be my first opportunity to hear the ambassador speak. It was the Mission's annual Independence Day event at the United Nations, and dozens of ambassadors were expected to attend along with many other invited guests. Avishai had written the remarks and together we walked over to Ron's office to review them. Ron was in a jovial mood, having just returned from a trip to China. All smiles, he scanned the speech and told us it was fine. I later learned it was rarely that easy to get a speech approved.

The coming weeks were mostly memorable for their baffling introduction to Israeli work culture. At a security briefing for English-speaking employees, the security head advised that, in the event of an emergency, instructions would be announced over the building intercom. The security guard leading the briefing candidly offered, "If it's a real emergency, the guys probably won't remember to translate instructions. I can offer two pieces of advice. Learn Hebrew or just follow the crowd."

Sometimes, my questions sent colleagues into fits of laughter. Early on, I asked our chief of staff, Ella, for the policy papers that would lay out the positions on various issues, so I could ensure that everything I wrote was consistent with government policies. Working for the Ontario government, I had frequently referenced the governing party's platform and position papers. My request for policy papers turned out to be the most amusing question I ever asked Ella. To this day, she laughs when reminded of the nervous Canadian that stood before her timidly asking for a set of position papers. I quickly learned it wasn't simple to know where the government stood on any given issue. Israel's government is built around a coalition of minority political parties. Unlike the Canadian or American governments, where Cabinet members will usually adhere to the party's platform, Israeli policies are something of a free-for-all. Ask a group of Israeli Cabinet members for their position on Jerusalem, for example. Some will say it is the eternal, undivided capital of Israel, while others believe it should be divided, with East Jerusalem becoming the capital of a future Palestinian state.

In my first year at the Mission, I also learned a great deal about how Israelis approach protocol. The first time I was asked to write a *note verbale*, I turned to Google to understand what was being requested. The search engine described it as a diplomatic note that is, "more formal than an aide-mémoire and less formal than a note, drafted in the third person and never signed." The definition was probably written by the Israeli Foreign Ministry's Human Resources department. I found an example of a *note verbale* in Nate's old files and proceeded to draft a letter in the same format. At the top was a curious combination of letters and numbers. I asked a colleague what numbers I should put on the top of the note and he said, "Just make it up."

"Make it up?" I asked in disbelief. "Doesn't the number serve a purpose of some sort?"

"Not for us, we just make them up," he cheerfully replied.

Far be it for me to argue for a more logical system. I shrugged and decided to assign *note verbale* numbers based on my mood. I used 24601—*Les Misérables*'s Jean Valjean's prisoner number—when I felt captive to my workload. On a particularly frustrating day, I unleashed a double license to kill, placing 007007 at the top of the note.

In time, I grew used to the abrupt and demanding culture and learned to similarly maneuver around some of the more tedious office procedures. Our weekly staff meetings, for example, were painfully slow. The entire staff would cram into a boardroom sized to fit about half of us and each person would offer an update on his or her work, and an agonizingly long discussion would follow. The meetings dragged on for hours, forcing me to work late into the evening to make up the lost time. After a few months, I decided the meetings were a colossal waste of my time and simply stopped attending. I expected to be instructed to return or at the very least be asked why I stopped going. When I was finally asked after weeks of missing meetings, I shrugged and said I didn't understand the Hebrew. Nobody questioned me, even when it was clear that my Hebrew was perfectly adequate.

By far, the most challenging aspect of my job was learning to amend the tone of my writing. I had been raised in Canada, employed in government, and was—at least when I started working for Israel's Ministry of Foreign Affairs—polite, soft-spoken, and politically correct. The Israelis immediately began my reeducation. I would draft materials only to have them returned with instructions to be less apologetic and more acerbic. The very first letter I was asked to write was to a catering company that had charged an incorrect corporate credit card. I drafted a letter explaining the error and asking for the charge to be reversed and placed on a different card.

Soon after I submitted it for review, a colleague came to find me. Handing it back, she shook her head and said, "This will never do. You need to be far more aggressive."

"Aggressive?" I asked, perplexed. "It's just a processing error."

Narrowing her eyes, she grimly responded, "With that attitude, how will they ever learn?"

On top of the foreign work culture, I had to learn the unique language of my new boss. This turned out to be the most daunting challenge. I would prepare a draft of a speech, hand it to him for review, and wait nervously for his verdict. If he pronounced something "snooze, snooze," he was saying it was boring. If he wanted more cynicism, he would proclaim, "shove it to them!" And when he wanted new ideas in his speeches, he would declare, "Engage the brain!"

The "snooze, snooze" problem could oftentimes be addressed by finding an interesting quote, particularly if it came from Winston Churchill, whom he admired enormously. In my first weeks at work, I heard Ron deliver remarks at an event honoring Israel's sixty-fifth Independence Day that included a particularly fitting quote about turning sixty-five:

Winston Churchill once said that "sixty-five is the age when you wake up in the morning—looking forward to a nap in the afternoon." Yet . . . at age sixty-five, the Start-Up Nation is just getting started. In just six decades,

Israel has moved from harvesting apples to designing Apple computers;
from planting trees in the desert to putting companies on the NASDAQ
stock exchange.

Impressed, I remarked to a colleague that it was tremendous luck to find
such a fitting quote from Churchill.

Grinning, she replied, "Not really. It was a made-up quote."

Seeing my stunned expression, she explained, "Ron thought the speech
was dull and told us to find a Churchill quote." She shrugged and continued,
"For all we know, Winston Churchill *could* have said that line. Not everything is recorded for posterity."

Ron insisted his speeches be peppered with jokes and biting one-liners.
Before starting at the mission, I read through all his old speeches delivered
in the United Nations and they were chock full of cheesy lines, à la:

You don't have to be a rocket scientist to understand that if rockets fall on
your head, you have a right to defend yourself.

It doesn't take an architect to recognize how poorly Palestinians have laid
the foundations for statehood in the West Bank and Gaza Strip.

It does not take an NYPD detective—or Sherlock Holmes—to see that the
fingerprints of senior PA officials were all over the recent provocations.

The European Union continues to define Hezbollah as a charitable and
political group, not a terrorist organization. This is no less ridiculous than

describing the Mafia as a chamber of commerce or the Ku Klux Klan as a gentleman's social club.

Asking the Iranian regime to take part in developing solutions for Syria is like inviting the Mafia to head the murder investigation squad of the NYPD.

Putting Iran and Syria on a Human Rights Council is like putting the Godfather in charge of a witness-protection program.

For the most part, I thought these jokes were silly and juvenile. I assumed they reflected a frat boy sense humor on the part of preceding speechwriters, and I swore I would write far more sophisticated jokes. Wrong. My new boss loved, and I mean *loved*, cheesy one-liners and insisted on having them in almost all of his speeches. By the time I left the Mission, I had written hundreds and will readily admit that quite a few were far more groanworthy than anything that had come before me.

When I first started at the Mission, I struggled terribly to come up with gag lines. Thankfully, Avishai easily channeled Ron's brand of humor. After I drafted a speech, we would sit together and brainstorm caustic wisecracks to pepper throughout the text. When we came up with something that seemed particularly asinine to me and humorous to him, we knew we had a winner.

Earlier this month, Hamas police pulled dozens of young men off the street and brutally beat them for the so-called "offense" of wearing pants that were too tight. I'd say that this is taking the phrase "fashion police" to a whole new level.

[SPEECH TO THE SECURITY COUNCIL ON THE
SITUATION IN THE MIDDLE EAST, APRIL 2013]

Hamas manages a wide array of groups claiming to be social services orga-
nizations. I suppose if you consider laundering money a way of "cleaning
up the neighborhood," then this is accurate.

[SPEECH TO THE SECURITY COUNCIL ON
COUNTERTERRORISM, MAY 2013]

You don't need a PhD in geography to understand that a map of the Middle
East that omits any mention of the state of Israel, is a scandal.

[LETTER TO THE SECRETARY GENERAL
REGARDING THE UNITED NATIONS RELIEF AND
WORKS AGENCY FOR PALESTINE REFUGEES
IN THE NEAR EAST (UNRWA), MAY 2013]

Syria is an academy for terrorists. It teaches the philosophy of fundamental-
ism, the engineering of explosives, and the calculus of chaos.

[SPEECH TO THE SECURITY COUNCIL ON
COUNTERTERRORISM, NOVEMBER 2013]

In time, it got easier to write in the expected style, but I did on one occasion
seriously overachieve. I was asked to write a letter following an incident in
which an IDF jeep was fired upon from a military outpost inside Syria. It
was the fifth time Syrian forces had shot at Israel from the same position.
The IDF retaliated by firing back and destroying the military outpost.
Outraged, the Syrian delegation sent a furious letter to the Security Council
condemning Israel for fomenting unrest.

I was instructed to write a letter to the Security Council explaining Israel's
actions. I sat down at my computer and did my best to channel righteous
indignation. When I was done, I took the letter to Ron. When he finished

reading, he looked up at me and calmly said, "Klompas, I think you have declared war on Syria in this letter."

In that moment I was entirely unsure if I had failed miserably or finally hit a homerun. Sensing my uncertainty, he handed back the letter and continued, "And to be clear, Canada, you are not authorized to declare war on anyone." I silently wondered what rank I needed to be to declare war.

———————————

Finding the right balance in my writing was an ongoing struggle. Ron wanted to deliver a speech that would make splashy headlines tomorrow, while I had grandiose dreams of writing a speech that would stand the test of time, replete with lines that would one day be chiseled on a stone monument as a testament to the wisdom and eloquence of its author. It was like getting a bucket of cold water dumped on me each time I was asked to write a gag line that began with "It doesn't take a . . . "

The same problem arose when it came to writing op-eds. Ron would call me at all hours of the day and night with an idea for a piece that he wanted published in a prestigious national newspaper. One of the first requests I got was to write about a UN resolution introduced by Israel entitled "Entrepreneurship for Development." Entirely non-political, the resolution encouraged governments to invest in entrepreneurs and create policies that can enable new businesses to take root and flourish.

Few countries know more about reaping wealth from entrepreneurship than Israel. Nicknamed the Start-Up Nation, Israel is small in size, with few natural resources, dry and arid farming conditions, and persistent adversity. Israel's regional isolation has compelled its citizens to become creative problem solvers and the country's small size promotes collaboration and the exchange of ideas. In Israel, there aren't six degrees of separation, there are just one or two. On top of this, compulsory military service exposes young adults to high-stakes situations, forcing them to assume weighty responsibility early in life. Following their service, they carry these leadership skills into the world along with a tested tolerance for risk-taking. Finally, the secret sauce may well be a start-up culture that views failure as a helpful, possibly even necessary, building block to success. The result is that Israel is today a member of the Organization for Economic Co-operation and Development (OECD) and a global leader in innovation, with one of the highest numbers of start-ups and patents per capita of any country.

As soon as our delegation introduced the entrepreneurship resolution, the Arab bloc launched a campaign calling on member states to oppose the measure. When this failed to gain traction, they sought to thwart the resolution by introducing politically charged language. Disgusted by the politicization, Ron instructed me to write an op-ed that could run in one of the country's major newspapers. Thoroughly unimpressed with the first tempered draft I wrote, he instructed me to get tough and write it again. I redrafted the article with an excess of gibes:

> When it comes to the Arab League, however, the situation remains stifling. For years they have employed theatrics on the U.N.'s global stage to condemn Israel. Using techniques only a contortionist could appreciate, they have stretched the truth and bent over backwards to embed anti-Israel vitriol in even the most benign of statements . . . The Middle East is dripping in oil wealth, but millions of people are starved of their basic rights and freedoms . . . The Arab world has thus far adopted the ostrich technique; heads buried in the sand, they are hoping the problem will go away on its own.

Ron was finally satisfied, but I knew no top-tier newspaper would publish an article with so many trite and gimmicky barbs. Try as we might, Avishai and I could not convince Ron to moderate the tone. Avishai shared the article with an editor friend at the *Wall Street Journal*. We hoped he would offer the constructive feedback we needed to convince Ron the writing style had to change. The op-ed ended up in front of the paper's foreign affairs columnist and a Pulitzer Prize laureate. He wrote back to us saying, "The point is certainly correct, but too many hackneyed phrases." We got the feedback we'd hoped for, but what a price to pay; Bret Stephens called my writing hackneyed.

CHAPTER 3

Lo nora / It's not so terrible

What do you mean I have to be a mind reader?

Every month the UN Security Council holds a debate titled "The situation in the Middle East, including the Palestinian Question." If the content of these sessions more accurately dictated the title, it would be called: "The Palestinian Injustice! And if we have time, some other stuff happening in the region."

I joined the Israeli Mission at the height of the Arab Spring. Protests and demonstrations crisscrossing the Middle East and North Africa had begun in late 2010, when a female Tunisian police officer confiscated the cart of a twenty-six-year-old street vendor named Mohamed Bouazizi, slapped him in the face, and demanded a bribe to return the cart. The young man had previously been harassed by local officials, but this time didn't have the money to pay the expected bribe. Without the cart, he had no means to support his widowed mother and six siblings. Humiliated at his treatment by a woman and distraught, Bouazizi stood outside the headquarters of the provincial government and lit himself on fire. Outraged by the corruption and abuse of power that had led a young man to take such desperate action, protests erupted in the rural town of Sidi Bouzid, Tunisia, and soon spread across the country. A month later, President Zine El Abidine Ben Ali fled the country. Mohamed Bouazizi became a symbol for millions of men and women in the

Arab world who longed for freedom and opportunity. The anger and frustration of ordinary people throughout the region boiled over and they took to the streets in protest.

When I joined the Israeli Mission, the Middle East was in chaos. Civil war was raging in Syria, Libya was on the brink of collapse, Iraq was faltering, Yemen was in turmoil, and ISIS's power was growing. These crises should have been the focus of international attention, particularly in debates devoted to the situation in the Middle East, but the Security Council's time was overwhelmingly spent discussing the Israeli-Palestinian conflict.

Every Middle East debate begins with a briefing from the UN's Special Coordinator for the Middle East Peace Process. I would listen as he itemized, in excruciating detail, a long list of Israeli infractions. He denounced settlements, expressed grave concern for raids and arrests, and voiced alarm over house demolitions. He also had a penchant for laboriously detailing the whereabouts of Palestinian olive trees that had been uprooted or vandalized.

The special coordinator then moved on to addressing the Palestinians' transgressions, but did so in a manner that was wrapped in a cautious cushion of doubt. He would report Palestinians had *allegedly* thrown stones at Israeli cars, or Israeli forces *claimed* a settlement had been infiltrated by armed terrorists, or Palestinians had *supposedly* caused unrest in Jerusalem by throwing firebombs at police.

We joked there were two consistent features of the Security Council's Middle East reports—they were long, and they were wrong. Or at least egregiously one-sided.

Every third month, the Israeli and Palestinian ambassadors were invited to deliver remarks to the Security Council. These debates were covered extensively in the Israeli media and, from the point of view of the Israeli delegation, were an opportunity to try and correct the record. Countless hours went into preparing these speeches. Following Nate's departure, Avishai stepped in as substitute speechwriter and began preparing a first draft of the first Middle East speech, which he dutifully turned over to me to complete. The diplomat at the Mission primarily responsible for providing the content of these speeches was fittingly named Israel.

For the sake of clarity, I'll call him Israel-the-diplomat to distinguish him from Israel-the-country. Tall, broad-shouldered, and prematurely greying at the temples, Israel-the-diplomat was intelligent, insightful, and hardworking. He was usually last to leave the office late at night, and it was most common to see him either running to a meeting or huddled behind mountains of teetering papers in his office. Israel-the-diplomat was well-respected by his colleagues at the United Nations. This was even true for diplomats who didn't look kindly on Israel-the-country.

When I needed to get his thoughts on the content for the quarterly Middle East speech, I would jog alongside him as he rushed between meetings and scribble notes as he rattled off a list of topics, "Make sure you cover Iran, the Palestinians, incitement, Hezbollah—you *must* mention Hezbollah. And I want resolution 1701 and double war crimes. Do not leave out the double war crimes."

Israel-the-diplomat's list of topics didn't vary much between the Middle East speeches. Fortunately, Ron and Ella also provided a robust list of topics they wanted included. They were a powerful combination. Ron was politically astute, and Ella had a keen ability to discern patterns in current events. Together, we would work to shape each Middle East speech around a timely theme.

About two weeks before my first Situation in the Middle East speech, Avishai and I took a draft of the remarks to Ron for review. He read it through and said, "I'm not married to any of this," as he handed the papers back to me. Avishai stood to leave and I followed him.

"What does that mean?" I asked, once we were out of Ron's office.

"Don't worry," Avishai reassured me. "If he really didn't like it, you'd know. It's early. There will be a lot more changes coming."

Every day I distributed a new draft to senior staff. They would send back conflicting instructions and rambling suggestions for new sections. I'd work late into the night trying to capture their directions. At ten o'clock one evening, Ella, Avishai, and I sat huddled around my computer while Nate, who had relocated to California, dictated his edits and comments over the phone in his customary rapid-fire staccato manner. The following evening, a similar scene repeated. Eventually, it got so late that the security team shooed us out of the building. Far from done, we relocated to a coffee shop down the street, huddled around a laptop, and continued working.

As the day of the Middle East speech approached, senior staff argued over which sections should be removed or reworded and what topics should get added. By this point, we had gone through twenty drafts of the speech and there was still no end in sight. When I complained it was impossible to satisfy all the conflicting opinions, Ella sat me down and explained, "There is only one opinion that counts, and it belongs to the guy sitting in the corner office."

With that in mind, I went alone to Ron with the latest draft of the speech. He read each page aloud and every now and then took his pen and scratched out entire paragraphs or put the pages down and dictated new sections. Satisfied, I went to my office and made the changes. The following day, I brought him a clean draft. I was dismayed to see him reach for his pen and once again, scratch out sections. We repeated this exercise each time. Vexingly, entire pages he had praised one day, were summarily dismissed as poorly written or no longer relevant the following day.

Two days before the speech, I had written twenty-five drafts of the speech. It dawned on me with considerable dismay that the remarks would not be finished until Ron read them to the Security Council. The morning of the speech, I printed a clean draft and, with Avishai at my side, went to Ron. Sitting at his desk, he read through slowly and asked for some changes. We were about a page and half from finishing when his phone rang. He picked up the phone and swiveled around in his chair. Avishai and I stepped out of the room and stood by Dafna's desk, watching as he settled back in his large leather desk chair and got lost in conversation. My eyes darted impatiently between the back of Ron's chair and my watch as the clock ticked ever closer to ten o'clock when the debate was scheduled to start.

At ten minutes to ten, Ron hung up the phone, stood up, grabbed his UN badge and strode past us saying, "Time to go."

We watched his back retreat down the hall. I turned to Avishai and said, "Hopefully that last page didn't require any changes." We ran to my office to make the final edits and printed fresh copies of the speech. Avishai rushed off to make copies for the UN interpreters and together we dashed to the UN building one block away. We weaved through the corridors and arrived outside the Security Council chamber. With a deep breath, I pulled open the door and walked across the room and handed Ron the speech just as the session began.

The UN complex was being renovated at the time, and a temporary Security Council had been built to replicate the iconic chamber. Ron sat calmly at the horseshoe-shaped wooden table. Directly behind him sat our deputy ambassador and beside him, Israel-the-diplomat. Ella and I took the two seats behind them. Avishai had warned me that Ron often wanted last minute changes or additions to his speech. He would slip a note back and expect his speechwriter to hand back text he could add to his speech within a minute or two. I waited tensely.

The session began with the special coordinator's briefing and was followed by a twenty-minute diatribe against Israel from the Palestinian ambassador, Riyad Mansour. As Mansour began his remarks, a UN official walked around the room handing out copies of his remarks. Ron flipped through the pages of Mansour's speech, scanned the text, and homed in on a section. He grabbed a piece of paper, hastily scribbled a note, and passed it back to me.

A draft of the speech I had written days earlier included a section detailing how the Palestinian Authority was abusing humanitarian funding from the Norwegian government. Oslo was sending payments to the Palestinian Authority to support the families of convicted terrorists held in Israeli prisons. However, those funds never reached the intended family members because the Palestinian government funneled the money directly to prisoners as a reward for their terrorist acts. Palestinian ambassador Mansour's speech included a section thanking Oslo for its support. Ron intended to enlighten the Norwegians as to exactly how their aid dollars were being spent.

We had cut that paragraph of the speech to get the speech down to twenty minutes. Now Ron wanted it back. Ella's quick thinking saved the day. She searched through her emails, retrieved an old version of the speech and found the relevant section. I took a clean piece of notepaper, copied the text, and passed it forward to Ron moments before it was his turn to speak.

As Ron began his remarks, I finally sat back and absorbed the scene. I looked at each of the ambassadors sitting around the table. Above us was a replica of the famous mural of a phoenix rising from the ashes. Off to the side, the interpreters sat in their booths alongside the official photographers and videographers, who recorded the sessions for posterity. Behind us, the gallery was filled with delegates, and behind them, members of the public. Awed by my surroundings, I turned my attention to Ron and listened as he read the words Avishai and I had written.

Last Tuesday, the State of Israel marked sixty-five years as a free and independent homeland for the Jewish people. On that historic day six-and-a-half decades ago, the leaders of the new Jewish state issued a Declaration of Independence. It affirmed (and I quote), "We offer peace and unity to all the neighboring states and their peoples and invite them to cooperate with the independent Jewish nation for the common good of all."

Israel wants peace. Not a day has gone by in the past sixty-five years in which the people of Israel have not yearned for peace. Last month, during his visit to Israel, President Obama said, "I know Israel has taken risks for peace . . . [and] I believe that the Israeli people do want peace."

Jewish tradition teaches that the world is sustained on three pillars—truth, justice, and peace. Today I'd like to speak about the three pillars upon which a true and lasting peace in our region must stand. These pillars of peace are the foundation that must remain standing in the shifting sands of the Middle East.

[EXCERPT OF SITUATION IN THE
MIDDLE EAST DEBATE, APRIL 2013]

When Ron finished reading his speech, Ella leaned over and instructed me to return to the office and circulate the remarks to the media. I slid out of my seat and walked to the door. Pausing, I took one last look around the room and slipped out. Avishai followed and together we walked back to the office and got to work distributing the press release. Later that afternoon, Avishai appeared at my door with a yellow frosted cupcake and a smile. He placed the colorful dessert on my desk and said, "You survived. It'll get easier."

During my tenure, I heard Israeli representatives deliver over one hundred speeches I had written to UN bodies. Every time, no matter how exhausted or cranky or stressed I was feeling, a sense of exhilaration washed over me when I heard words I had penned being delivered by Israel's representatives to the United Nations.

———

In addition to working on the Middle East speech, I had a lengthy list of Ron's community speaking engagements. He accepted three to five invitations each week, on top of the speeches he delivered in the United Nations, and it didn't matter the length, location, or audience: Ron insisted every speech be engaging, humorous, and persuasive.

While it wasn't always easy for him to express what he wanted in his speeches, Ron was utterly clear about what he didn't want. When a new speech was added to the schedule, I would check if he had an idea in mind and he would usually instruct me to collect my ideas into a first draft. When I presented the draft, odds are he would lambast me for shoddy ideas or poor writing. Worse, he would frequently harangue me after reading just a paragraph or two. I didn't have time to go to the gym, but I engaged in plenty of exercises in futility. On one occasion, I had written dozens of drafts of a speech. Not satisfied with any of them, Ron irritably dictated word for word what he wanted me to write. When I returned with the typed text, he looked at the page and snapped, "I know that's what I told you to write, but it's not what I meant!"

Utterly exasperated, I shot back, "Ron, I'm your speechwriter, not a mind reader or a miracle worker." With a smirk, he handed back the speech and sent me out of the office with instructions to think of a new angle. That evening, I called Nate and asked how he had survived in this job. He laughed and told me his first six months had been a nightmare.

"Come to think of it," he said, "I think I blocked that time from my mind. It was too traumatic." He continued, "I can tell you this, you'll get better and it will become easier. It will never be easy, but it will get easier."

Hardly mollified, I complained that Ron was being completely unreasonable. Nate laughed again and said, "Ron will be the first to admit that he is unreasonable. But he is also one of the most decent people you will ever meet." Nate finished by saying, "In time, he will grow to trust you and then you will find that you have never had a better ally or friend." I didn't believe it at the time, but it was true.

One of the first community speeches I prepared for Ron was a briefing for a group of New York rabbis. In the days leading up to the event, I had written countless drafts, each of which Ron deemed inadequate. The morning of the speech, I presented him with yet another draft as we walked to the car that would take us to the event. He settled into his seat and flipped through the remarks before shaking his head irritably and handing the pages back to me.

We arrived at the venue and Ron stepped out of the car, buttoned his jacket, and bounded energetically up the steps. Dafna and I trailed behind into a large room packed with excited guests. Ron went from table to table, shaking hands, and affably agreeing to be photographed with anyone who asked. Before long, he was introduced by the event organizer. Dafna and I found seats at the back of the room and settled in to listen. For thirty minutes Ron held the group spellbound, speaking animatedly without once glancing at notes. He was completely at ease in front of an audience, captivating them with humorous quips and insights into current events.

The audience listened in pin-drop silence as he explained the institutionalized bias of the United Nations' Geneva-based Human Rights Council. He explained that every year, the council singles out Israel alone for individual criticism.

"When it comes time to vote on these biased resolutions," Ron began, "who always stands by our side?" He paused before answering his own question, "The great kingdom of Palau!" The audience tittered. Odds are most of them had never heard of the archipelago in the western Pacific Ocean, nor knew it consistently voted in support of Israel, but Ron's jovial enthusiasm had them captivated. and they tittered.

Ron continued: "And why is Israel singled out from all the countries in the world? Are we not even good enough to be with a group that includes Syria, Iran, and North Korea? Oh no, the UN gives us a category all our own. This isn't a double standard; it's a triple standard—one standard for democracies, one standard for dictatorships, and a special, impossible standard for Israel."

The audience was hanging on his every word. Ron launched into one of his favorite stories about the infighting at the United Nations and the audience exploded in laughter. Fired up, he regaled the room with backroom anecdotes for another fifteen minutes. When he was done, Ron looked seriously at his audience and said, "I want to say thank you. Receiving a thank you from an Israel representative is unheard of, so cherish the moment."

With that, he bounded off the stage. Dafna jumped to her feet and instructed me to get my coat. We fell in step with Ron as he strode down the aisle and made a beeline for the door, pausing momentarily to grab a bagel from the refreshment table.

When we were settled in the car, I turned to Ron and exclaimed, "Why did you give me such a hard time? You didn't need a speech at all!"

He chuckled, picked up his phone, and started scrolling through his messages. "Klompas, you will learn. Let's go to Starbucks."

Starbucks was a prominent part of my life as Ron's speechwriter. Almost every outing began or ended with a visit to Starbucks. Baristas within a mile radius of the office knew him as the Grande, single shot latte guy. Ron would always instruct the barista that he was paying for whatever was ordered by his staff. Warm drinks in hand, we would shuffle out the door, back into the car, and continue to our next stop.

While it was hit-or-miss as to whether Ron would read his drafted remarks when he spoke in the community, he would almost certainly read word for word the text of his UN speeches. I once accompanied him to the Security Council to deliver a speech on counterterrorism. Later in the afternoon I was in my office when Dafna called and announced, "I'm connecting you to Ron."

A few seconds later, Ron was on the line demanding to know why I had removed the line from the speech about Mother Teresa, or as he called her, "Mama Teresa."

I had no clue what he was talking about, but years of working in government positions had taught me the virtues of murmuring a few vague sentences and asking a couple of probing questions. From what I could gather, it seemed someone had distributed a press release to the Hebrew-language media which had no bearing on the remarks Ron had actually delivered to the Security Council. The release included a quote about Mother Teresa and Ron was under the impression the speech he had approved for delivery had referenced Mother Teresa but had been cut from the version he read to the Council.

I tried to set the record straight.

"Ron, there was never a reference to Mother Teresa in any draft of the speech."

"There was," he stubbornly insisted.

"I wrote every word of every draft and I can tell you with utter certainty that there was never any mention of Mother Teresa."

Ron was quiet for a moment and then harangued me for not understanding that he had wanted Mother Teresa in his speech. "Klompas, you have to get inside my mind."

"Ron," I started with a sigh, "If that's what you want, then I will work on learning to read your mind."

Delighted, he replied, "That's all I ask for!" and hung up.

A minute later the phone rang. I answered and Dafna pronounced, "I'm connecting you to Ron."

I waited tensely, expecting a further berating.

Ron got on the line and announced, "Aviva!"

"Yes, Ron?" I asked cautiously.

"Where does the expression, 'The proof is in the pudding,' come from?"

I wondered what sort of insane psychological games this man was playing with me.

"I have no idea, Ron."

"Well, find out. I'm having lunch with someone and we are discussing the issue," he replied.

Cradling the phone with my chin, I quickly typed the phrase into Google and read aloud what I found.

"Good. Keep researching and get back to me." he declared before hanging up.

Baffled, I stared at the phone for a few seconds and decided the best course of action was to get far, far away from the phone. I went to look for Ella and found her in the boardroom eating lunch. I slumped down into a chair across from her and indignantly complained that someone had screwed up the press release. Ella had no interest in my whining. Barely glancing up from her salad, she responded with a simple "*lo nora,*" which is Hebrew for "It's not so terrible," and sent me on my way.

Ron's speechwriter really did have to be something of a mind reader because his instructions could be downright cryptic. He might, for example, ask for a speech to include "the bit about the train." This referred to a favorite metaphor used to explain Iran's nuclear ambitions:

> *The Iranian nuclear program continues to advance at the speed of an express train. The international community's efforts to stop them are moving at the pace of the local train, pausing at every stop for some nations to get off and on.*

Or he might ask for the "King Hussein story" to illustrate responsible leadership in the Middle East:

> *Fifteen years after his death, King Hussein's legacy of peace lives on. Israelis from across the political and religious spectrum still admire King Hussein's*

*towering morality and his profound belief in the sanctity of life and the
dignity of every human being.*

*We will never forget the sight of King Hussein consoling the Israeli families
whose children had been killed in a terrorist attack. After learning that a
Jordanian soldier had murdered seven Israeli schoolgirls, King Hussein
traveled to Israel to visit the homes of the bereaved families. One by one, he
sat with the grieving parents, held their hands, offered words of condolence
and hugged and kissed them.*

*King Hussein told them (and I quote), "I feel that if there is anything left
in life, it will be to ensure that all the children enjoy the kind of peace and
security that we never had in our times."*

Eventually I became fairly decent at reading Ron's mind. I developed a sense
of what he would appreciate and what he would dismiss out of hand. I
learned to channel his brand of humor and could decipher his one or two-
word shorthand prompts for his favorite anecdotes. Even so, it could still feel
like I was engaged in a complicated game of Mad Libs. I would hand Ron a
speech and he would rattle off a long and assorted hodgepodge of additions.
On one occasion, he had a particularly long set of additions for a speech on
entrepreneurship and development. Scanning the list, I shook my head in
wonder, before sending a quick email to Nate.

Subject: In case you miss us

Just went through Ron's entrepreneurship speech.
He likes it, but asked that I include the
following:

```
Peres joke, lighthouse, U.N. bureaucracy joke,
Rudyard Kipling quote (you'll be a Man, my son!),
beg forgiveness from society, ice cutter (with
metaphor of how it paves the way), marathon vs
sprint and end with a better world.
```

```
Living the dream!
```

I would spend hours trying to work Ron's potpourri of ideas into his speeches, while still ensuring the text flowed smoothly. The task was made easier if I "forgot" some of the more abstract ideas. There was a fifty-fifty chance he would recall the missing element, and if he did, he would certainly scold my carelessness.

Sometimes the final product was admittedly a bit muddled, but much to my surprise, the speeches usually turned out stronger thanks to Ron's creative embellishments. Of course, I would never give him the satisfaction of admitting as much.

In addition to writing Ron's speeches, I was tasked with managing much of the Mission's English language communications. This included speeches for half a dozen other diplomats in the delegation and countless visiting dignitaries. There were also opinion articles, letters, press releases, and a fair amount of social media content. It was far more work than one person could manage alone, and I was grateful to have Avishai and the help of a part-time intern. Even with their assistance, I was working late into the night and camping out in coffee shops with my laptop on weekends.

Every day, someone would pop their head into my office and instruct me to write a speech for one of the United Nations' six committees. In a week, I could find myself writing on a challenging array of topics: sustainable development, counter-terrorism, peacekeeping, global health, sports, outer space, forestry, road safety, renewable energy, and much, much more.

The requests for writing support poured in, and I learned it was largely futile to ask to be provided with content. If I did hazard the question, the requester would give me a pointed look, as if it was pure laziness on my part to expect them to provide substantive content for their speeches. If pressed, they would generally send me a speech delivered in a previous session and instruct me not to reinvent the wheel. I used the old speeches to clue me in to key topics and set an intern to work gathering fresh data from think tanks, government reports, and research institutes. Poring over the research very often took longer than writing the speech.

For this reason, I loved working with Noa, our diplomat to the United Nations' Third Committee on human rights. Small, wiry, and intensely focused, Noa was intelligent, hard-working, and a master of her subject matter. She also had no ego, a rarity in a diplomat. Noa read endless reports, corresponded with experts in NGOs, and wheedled information from her contacts in Jerusalem. When we needed a speech on human rights, she would arrive in my office carrying a towering stack of reports. She would plop down in a chair beside my desk and delve into the subject matter, ideas tumbling out of her head faster than I could record them. As she spoke, she habitually pushed her glasses up the bridge of her nose, only to have them slip down as she bent over to scan through her notes.

In my first week on the job, it was Noa who came barreling into my office and, in the typically abrupt manner of an Israeli, demanded, "Why would you leave a calm and comfortable government job in Canada to come here and work around the clock for one of the most unpopular countries in the world?" She ended her question by saying, "*hishtagat?*" which is Hebrew for, "*Are you crazy?*"

I had been staring dejectedly at the jam-packed speech schedule and her question did nothing to raise my spirits. In addition to the long hours, my new colleagues were loud, stubborn, demanding, and had an unsettling habit of saying exactly what was on their minds.

One of the early speeches Noa and I worked on together was for a Security Council session. That week, I had a particularly heavy workload and was trying to finish writing a letter when Noa came into my office. I watched impatiently as she shuffled through her papers before finally digging out a factoid she wanted included in her speech. With obvious pride, she detailed the myriad ways Israel was upholding human rights and human dignity.

"Isn't that amazing?" she gushed.

I looked over her shoulder at the white board on my wall with its long lists of speeches and letters that needed to be written and muttered, "I don't know, I can think of at least one person who is currently enslaved by the State of Israel."

CHAPTER 4

Go'al nefesh /
Disgusting to the soul

How did we get here?

In 1952 Israel's first ambassador to the United Nations, Abba Eban, proposed an initiative for a cease-fire in Korea and was met with stubborn opposition in the global body. When Norway replaced Israel as the sponsor, the challenge was dropped, and the initiative passed. This sort of prejudicial treatment led Eban to famously quip: "If Algeria introduced a resolution declaring that the earth was flat and that Israel had flattened it, it would pass by a vote of 164 to 13 with 26 abstentions."

Not much has changed. If anything, anti-Israel bias has grown more pronounced as the decades have passed. Susan Rice spent five years as America's ambassador to the United Nations, and described the overt animosity toward Israel by saying, "The [United Nations] isn't at its best when it comes to Israel. In fact, it's sometimes at its worst."

Similarly, toward the end of his term as Secretary-General, Ban Ki-moon admitted, "Decades of political maneuvering have created a disproportionate number of resolutions, reports and committees against Israel. In many cases, instead of helping the Palestinian issue, this reality has foiled the ability of the [United Nations] to fulfill its role effectively."

The idea for the United Nations was conceived in a 1941 meeting between

American president Franklin Roosevelt and British prime minister Winston Churchill on a ship off the coast of Newfoundland. The United States had yet to formally enter World War II, and despite its official position of neutrality, it joined Great Britain in issuing a joint declaration that became known as the Atlantic Charter. They outlined a vision for an international institution to replace the faltering League of Nations, a global forum to mediate international conflicts and negotiate peace. Roosevelt suggested a name: The United Nations.

The governments of the United States, the Soviet Union, the United Kingdom, and China formalized the Atlantic Charter proposals shortly after the United States entered the War. In the "Declaration of the United Nations," these nations, along with twenty-two others, agreed to unite against the Axis powers and committed in principle to the establishment of a global body after the war.

Early in 1945, invitations were drafted to a conference that would take place in San Francisco to formally establish the United Nations. Days before the Conference was set to begin, President Roosevelt, whose health had been in decline, died of a cerebral hemorrhage. Vice President Harry Truman took the oath of office and announced the Conference would proceed as planned. Formally known as the United Nations Conference on International Organization, it opened on April 25, 1945, with delegates from fifty countries in attendance who represented over 80 percent of the world's population.

At the start of the conference, new American president Harry Truman addressed the assembled guests saying:

Delegates to the United Nations Conference on International Organization:

The world has experienced a revival of an old faith in the everlasting moral force of justice. At no time in history has there been a more important

Conference, or a more necessary meeting, than this one in San Francisco, which you are opening today . . . .

You members of this Conference are to be the architects of the better world. In your hands rests our future. By your labors at this Conference, we shall know if suffering humanity is to achieve a just and lasting peace . . .

If we do not want to die together in war, we must learn to live together in peace.

With firm faith in our hearts, to sustain us along the hard road to victory, we will find our way to a secure peace, for the ultimate benefit of all humanity.

We must build a new world—a far better world—one in which the eternal dignity of man is respected.

[ADDRESS BY PRESIDENT HARRY S. TRUMAN
TO THE UNITED NATIONS, APRIL 25, 1945]

For the next two months, delegations considered the structure and bodies for this new international organization, and drafted its charter. Every part of it had to be voted on and accepted by a two-thirds majority. On June 26, 1945, representatives of the fifty nations gathered to sign the charter and officially created the United Nations.

———————

Today's United Nations has fallen far short of the aspirations articulated by President Truman. When I joined the Israeli delegation in 2013, the number of member states in the United Nations stood at 193. Of them, just eighty-seven, or 45 percent, were democratic in nature.* In a twist of irony, dozens of nations that deny democratic rights to their own people abuse the United Nations' democratic forums to advance their political interests.

For Israel, the situation is even more challenging. Of the United Nations' 193 Member States, there are twenty-two Arab states and fifty-seven members of the Organisation of Islamic Cooperation, or OIC. Established in 1969 to unite Muslim states after the Six-Day War and describing itself as "the collective voice of the Muslim world," the OIC's opposition to Israel has long been a driving force of its existence. Its states belong to the two largest UN groupings, Africa and Asia, and often invoke bloc solidarity to isolate or pressure Israel.

Further stacking the odds against Israel is the 120-member strong Non-Aligned Movement or NAM. Founded by India, Indonesia, Egypt, Ghana, and the former Yugoslavia, NAM's members were first united by their desire to advocate for peaceful coexistence and their refusal to align with rivaling superpowers, the United States and the Soviet Union. The first NAM summit took place in Belgrade in 1961 at the height of the Cold War. Twenty-five countries were represented and the threat of war between the United States and the Soviet Union dominated the summit. Today, the NAM has 120-member states, representing nearly two-thirds of the United Nations' members and about 55 percent of the world population. This bloc has an automatic majority, because when the members of NAM vote as a bloc—120 members out of 193 UN member states—they easily pass any resolution.

From 2012 to 2016, Iran served as chair of NAM and used its position to bolster its allies and marginalize Israel. Late in 2016, the chairmanship of

---

* According to Freedom House, an independent watchdog organization dedicated to the expansion of freedom and democracy around the world.

NAM transferred to Venezuela at a summit attended by a veritable who's-who of autocratic leaders, including Zimbabwean president Robert Mugabe, Cuban president Raúl Castro, Palestine Authority president Mahmoud Abbas, and Iranian president Hassan Rouhani. Little changed with the transfer of chairmanship, as Venezuela is Iran's BFF—that is, it's best fanatical friend—ensuring ongoing hostility against Israel in the global institution.

The United Nations' bias against Israel is palpable in many of its committees, bodies, and agencies. Even the institution's membership structure has served to marginalize Israel. Member states belong to one of five regional groups: African Group, Asia-Pacific Group, Eastern European Group, Latin American and Caribbean Group, and the Western European and Others Group, more commonly known as WEOG. Unlike other groups, WEOG is not geographically based, but rather comprised of states with shared Western democratic values.

These regional groups facilitate elections to UN bodies, and serve as forums for consultations, negotiations, and voting decisions. By geographic right, Israel should belong to the Asia-Pacific Group, but some of its Arab members have flatly refused to admit the Jewish state.

In fact, for almost four decades Israel was the only country banned from joining a group. Without membership in a regional group, Israel could not be elected to agencies, councils, and committees like the Security Council, Human Rights Council, or the Economic & Social Council.

In 2000, fifty-one years after it was admitted to the United Nations system, WEOG offered to admit Israel to its regional group on a temporary basis, subject to renewal. It wasn't exactly throwing open the doors with a welcome celebration, as the offer came with conditions. Israel would not be allowed to present candidates for open seats in UN bodies, including on the

Security Council. The invitation also stipulated Israel would be considered an observer and denied the rights of a full member in WEOG discussions and consultations at the United Nations' offices in Geneva, Nairobi, Rome, and Vienna. Israel was finally offered membership in a regional group but was still being treated as a second-class member state. European states in WEOG were under pressure from Arab and other Islamic nations to tie Israel's acceptance into WEOG with concessions to the Palestinians. The United States urged Israel to accept the offer before its membership became a negotiating chip and promised it would immediately work to extend Israel's participation to Geneva. Recognizing this was the best deal on offer, Israel accepted the temporary membership. Four years later, Israel was granted indefinite renewal of its membership in WEOG's US headquarters. A decade later, on January 1, 2014, Israel was finally invited to join WEOG in Geneva, where the Human Rights Council is headquartered.

———

After the Security Council, the most well-known body at the United Nations is the General Assembly. It is the institution's main deliberative, policy-making, and representative organ, comprised of all 193 member states. In 2013, during the sixty-eighth session of the General Assembly, there were twenty-one resolutions singling out Israel for criticism. In comparison, there were only four condemnatory resolutions against other countries—one each on Syria, Iran, North Korea, and Myanmar. This appalling voting record would suggest Israel is twenty-one times worse than the regimes that drop barrel bombs on civilian neighborhoods, hang people from cranes in public squares, engage in modern-day slavery, and perpetrate ethnic cleansing. The global body's obsessive and politicized focus on Israel stands in stark contrast to its utter indifference to perennial perpetrators of grave violations of human rights, including nations where extrajudicial killings, sexual violence, torture, forced labor, and deliberate attacks on civilian areas take place.

Every year, the twenty or so resolutions singling out Israel pass by overwhelming majority, with the same states delivering rote accusations and regurgitating the language of old resolutions. The only countries to routinely oppose the resolutions are the United States, Canada, the Federated States of Micronesia, and Palau. Sometimes, Israel also enjoys the support of Australia and the Marshall Islands.

One annual resolution, for example, demands Israel compensate Lebanon for a 2006 oil spill. The resolution fails, of course, to clarify that hostilities began when Hezbollah launched rockets toward Israel and attacked a patrol unit, killing three soldiers and kidnapping two others, Ehud Goldwasser and Eldad Regev. Israel retaliated with air and sea attacks, one of which inadvertently struck oil storage tanks in Lebanon. The United Nations has never investigated the financial and environmental impact the thirty-three-day war had on Israel during which Hezbollah indiscriminately fired thousands of rockets. Israel cooperated closely with the UN Environment Program and other NGOs addressing the environmental situation along the coast of Lebanon. This good will has not earned Israel respite from its annual scolding. In 2014, while I was working for the Israeli delegation, the United Nations went one step further and demanded Israel pay Lebanon more than $850 million in compensation. The motion, which was not legally binding, passed with 170 countries voting in favor and just six—the United States, Canada, Australia, Micronesia, the Marshall Islands, and Israel—opposing.

During my first Fall General Assembly session, there was a single day in November when the General Assembly passed nine politically-motivated resolutions condemning Israel. One of these resolutions called on Israel to hand over the Golan Heights in Northern Israel to Syria. At the time, civil war in Syria had been raging for two and a half years and over 120,000 Syrian had been killed in the conflict. The United Nations was reporting extensively on the massacres taking place under Syrian president Bashar Al-Assad. Nonetheless, here was the global body demanding Israel hand territory and a civilian population over to the brutal Syrian regime. This resolution also passed with overwhelming support. For the most part, countries will adhere to their voting pattern from year to year with little regard to the evolving situation on the ground. The outbreak of the Syrian civil war and encroachment of ISIS on Israel's northern border did not dissuade countries from rubberstamping the annual condemnatory resolutions. The fact that Israel was, at the time, the only country to set up field hospitals to treat Syrian casualties of Assad's war against his own people similarly didn't cause countries to reconsider which nations serve to stabilize or destabilize the region.

And so it went. Resolution after resolution singled out Israel for censure. A Spanish-English interpreter sitting in the translation booth took note of the prejudicial focus on Israel. Not realizing her microphone was on and her remarks were broadcast into the earpiece of every UN delegate on the live webcast, she said as much to her colleague:

> *I think when you have . . . like a total of ten resolutions on Israel and Palestine, there's gotta be something, c'est un peu trop, non? [It's a bit much, no?] I mean I know . . . There's other really bad shit happening, but no one says anything about the other stuff.*
>
> [UN GENERAL ASSEMBLY INTERPRETER,
> NOVEMBER 13, 2013]

The delegates listened in silence and then burst into laughter. That rare moment of levity was quickly brushed aside as the delegates proceeded to vote and pass the nine resolutions against Israel.

Criticizing Israel's actions or policies is by no means anti-Semitic, but when the condemnation is grossly disproportionate, or Israel alone is repeatedly singled out, or the language of denunciation vile or tinged with libelous stereotype, then it's hard to see how the action is not discriminatory and anti-Semitic.

Questioning or denying Israel's right to exist as an equal member of the global community also points to a deeper bias. No one questions Russia or China's right to exist when they disagree with the policies of their governments. Why then is it acceptable for the Jewish state's legitimacy to be subject to discussion? Similarly, calling Israel or Israelis the "Zionist occupation forces" or to the "Zionist entity," as some Palestinian and Arab leaders are accustomed to doing, rather than use their internationally accepted names, denies the existence of the State and should be deemed unacceptable.

Another tactic is to deny Jewish history and assert that Jews are nothing more than colonizers. Palestinian Authority president Abbas has given speeches asserting that Israel grew out of a European colonial project that had nothing to do with Jewish history or aspirations.* In fact, the Jewish connection to Israel stretches back millennia. Zionism did not create a connection between Jews and the land of Israel, rather it is a political movement that champions Jewish self-determination in the land of Israel *because* it is the historical birthplace and biblical homeland of the Jewish people.

In 2016, former Assistant UN Secretary General Anthony Banbury wrote an op-ed for the *New York Times* explaining why he resigned his position. He

---

* Isabel Kershner, "Palestinian Leader Incites Uproar With Speech Condemned as Anti-Semitic," *New York Times*, May 2, 2018. https://www.nytimes.com/2018/05/02/world/middleeast/palestinians-abbas-israel-jews.html.

described colossal mismanagement compounded by minimal accountability, explaining, "If you locked a team of evil geniuses in a laboratory, they could not design a bureaucracy so maddeningly complex, requiring so much effort but in the end incapable of delivering the intended result. The system is a black hole into which disappear countless tax dollars and human aspirations, never to be seen again.*"

Banbury argued that too many decisions are driven by political expediency instead of by the values of the United Nations or the facts on the ground. This is certainly the case when it comes to the institution's treatment of Israel.

The United Nations Educational, Scientific, and Cultural Organization (UNESCO) is mandated with leading international cooperation in the fields of education, science, and culture. Its stated goal is to contribute to peace and security. Israel has had a checkered history with the organization. It joined in 1949 and was expelled in 1974 because of archaeological excavations on the Temple Mount that were deemed unacceptable by its members. Five years later, Israel was reinstated after the United States threatened to stop its funding of the organization. That hasn't stopped the body from attempting to erase Jewish history at the behest of its member states.

In 2010 the organization concluded that Rachel's Tomb, burial place of the biblical matriarch Rachel, was a mosque and called upon the Israeli government to remove the site along with the Tomb of the Patriarchs from its list of national heritage sites. In 2016 its Paris Executive Council adopted a Palestinian proposal that questioned the Jewish connection to the Temple Mount and the Western Wall in Jerusalem. Six months later, Algeria, Egypt, Lebanon, Morocco, Oman, Qatar, and Sudan submitted a resolution to UNESCO denying Israel's legal and historical rights anywhere in Jerusalem.

---

* Anthony Banbury, "I Love the U.N., but It Is Failing" *New York Times*, March 18, 2016. https://www.nytimes.com/2016/03/20/opinion/sunday/i-love-the-un-but-it -is-failing.html.

The vote, which coincided with Israel's Independence Day, passed with twenty-two countries in favor, twenty-three abstentions, ten opposed, and the representatives of three countries absent.

———————

Perhaps the worst anti-Israel bias can be found in Geneva at the United Nations' Human Rights Council. The body was established in 2006 to replace the UN Commission on Human Rights which was hopelessly indulgent of human rights abusers. The Commission was also hopelessly obsessed with denouncing Israel, but that fact didn't faze many champions of reform.

Things have not improved under the renamed, but similarly politicized, Human Rights Council. Freedom House is an NGO that rates the freedom of nations according to civil and political rights criteria. According to its 2018 rankings,* the Human Rights Council is comprised of twenty-one "free" states, twelve "partly free," and fourteen "not free." When it comes time to choose between national interests and human rights interests, politics wins every time.

The Human Rights Council has adopted more resolutions condemning Israel than the rest of the world combined. The Council's regular agenda of ten items reserves a permanent place, Agenda Item 7, to single out Israel— "Human rights situation in Palestine and other occupied Arab territories." In contrast, the Council addresses the human rights abuses of all countries in the world under Agenda Item 4.

No other country in the world—not Sudan which committed genocide, not Syria that is guilty of brutality and mass murder, and not North Korea that runs brutal forced labor camps—has its own standing agenda item. The result is that more than 50 percent of all condemnatory resolutions are

———————

* https://freedomhouse.org/report/freedom-world-2018-table-country-scores

directed at the Jewish state. Israel has also been the subject of more special sessions than any other state.

Between 2006 and 2014, the Human Rights Council issued 103 resolutions, fifty-six of which criticized Israel. Former American Ambassador to the UN Samantha Power described the injustice saying, "It is beyond absurd that the only country that has a standing place on the Human Rights Council's agenda is not Syria, not North Korea and not Iran, but Israel."

Overt anti-Israel bias appears to be a sought-after qualification for Council appointees. William Schabas was selected to head the United Nations' inquiry into the 2014 Gaza conflict between Israel and Hamas. His appointment came despite his record of public statements calling for the International Criminal Court to put Prime Minister Netanyahu and former president Shimon Peres on trial. Schabas eventually stepped down, but only after evidence emerged he had been paid to provide legal services to the Palestine Liberation Organization.

Two years later, the Human Rights Council appointed a "Special Rapporteur on the situation of human rights in the Palestinian territories occupied since 1967." The Council selected Canadian law professor Stanley Michael Lynk, who had a lengthy record of vocally criticizing Israel, including accusing it of "apartheid." At one point, he proposed solving the Israeli-Palestinian conflict by going "back to 1948, the date of partition and the start of ethnic cleansing."

The Council's bias against Israel can be shocking. In a March 2016 session, Palestinian foreign minister Riyad Maliki called on nations to refuse entry to settlers and "impose economic sanctions on the occupying entity." Here was a demagogue standing in the heart of Europe calling for the branding of Jewish businesses and the barring of Jewish people, and the delegates in attendance listened raptly. Three weeks later, the Council adopted Resolution 31/36 which calls for the United Nations to create a blacklist of companies operating in the West Bank, East Jerusalem, and the Golan

Heights. The council asked for the list of businesses to be updated annually and to be apprised of the "human rights and international law violations involved in the production of settlement goods." The motion passed with thirty-two nations voting in favor and fifteen abstentions. Not a single country on the Council voted against the motion.

The Council's obsessive focus on Israel means countless serious human rights situations around the world go unchallenged. While it would be unrealistic to expect a perfect balance in its human rights focuses, it is more than reasonable to conclude that the UN Human Rights Council's compulsive preoccupation with Israel has distracted it from fulfilling its mandate.

Another institution felled by politics is the United Nations Relief and Works Agency, or UNRWA. It was founded in 1949 as a temporary initiative to assist Palestine refugees following the Israeli-Arab conflict. Soon after, the United Nations established a High Commissioner for Refugees, or UNHCR, to serve as an all-encompassing international refugee agency to resettle those displaced by war. The two organizations never merged and so here we are seven decades later, and Palestinians continue to have their own distinct refugee agency.

The disparity between UNRWA and UNHCR is startling. Since its founding, UNHCR has helped over fifty million refugees successfully restart their lives, while UNRWA has not managed to diminish the problem of Palestinian refugees at all. To the contrary, the number of Palestinian refugees has ballooned from approximately seven hundred and fifty thousand in 1950 to over five million today.* Astoundingly, UNRWA does not have a mandate to resettle refugees; rather, its mandate is only to provide

---

*https://www.unrwa.org/palestine-refugees

assistance and as the population of Palestinian refugees grows, so does UNRWA's bureaucracy and budget.

According to the 1951 UN Convention and Protocol Relating to the Status of Refugees, a person is no longer a refugee if he or she has "acquired a new nationality and enjoys the protection of the country of his new nationality." UNRWA's definition of a Palestinian refugee includes no such provision. Under UNRWA's framework, Palestinians continue to be registered as refugees even after they acquire citizenship and find permanent housing. A Palestinian can be born in Qatar, live in Paris, hold a Swedish passport, and still be considered a refugee by UNRWA. Consider that, of the two million Palestinian refugees in Jordan, most have been granted Jordanian citizenship, yet UNRWA still counts them as refugees.

Another reason the number of Palestinian refugees is growing is Palestinians can pass their refugee status to their children and grandchildren. UNRWA registers as refugees "descendants of Palestine refugee males, including adopted children" even when there is no issue of the descendent being a refugee owing to a sound fear of being persecuted.

Palestinian refugees have been on the United Nations' permanent payroll for almost seventy years, and more are added with every passing generation. UNRWA demands enormous financial support from the international community to support education, health, and social services programs for this growing population. In 2013 UNHCR reported a staff of about nine and a half thousand personnel to support almost forty-three million refugees, internally displaced persons, and "others of concern" in more than one hundred countries.* Around the same time, UNRWA reported a staff of around thirty thousand personnel to support over five million persons in Jordan, Lebanon, Syria, the West Bank, and Gaza Strip.†

---

* https://www.unhcr.org/55f2c7099.pdf UNHCR staff is noted on page 16 as 9,411
† UNRWA, "In Figures as of 1 July 2014."

Although UNRWA receives some resources from the UN regular budget, most of its funding is provided through voluntary contributions. Scan the list of UNRWA's top contributors and you'll find it's almost exclusively North American and West European countries.* The Arab nations are the first to bemoan the plight of the Palestinian people, and the last to open their wallets.

In an effort to bring these issues to light, I frequently wrote statements, social media posts, and even an op-ed† describing how UNRWA exacerbates the conflict by embracing the Palestinians' demand for a "right of return." In its schools, teachers and textbooks educate Palestinian children that they will one day be repatriated to the villages their families left in 1948. UNRWA institutions display maps of 'Palestine' covering the entire geography of Israel. In doing so, UNRWA is fueling a Palestinian aspiration that greatly exceeds that which is reasonable or possible to achieve, thus perpetuating the conflict.

---

* Governments and EU Pledges to UNRWA's Programmes in 2017 https://www
.unrwa.org/sites/default/files/government_donors_and_eu_overall_ranking.pdf.
† https://www.jpost.com/Opinion/Op-Ed-Contributors/The-worlds-preferred
-refugees-317119.

CHAPTER 5

Chutzpa / Audacity

What is a global pastry of imagination?

Ron Prosor commands attention in a room through a combination of his stature, his deep resonating voice, and his charisma. Warm and genial, he is adept at putting people at ease with a joke or anecdote even in challenging circumstances. To be sure, Ron is tough and can be quick to anger, but he rarely holds a grudge, and is fiercely loyal to those who earn his respect.

Without question, he was the most demanding person I ever worked for. When the going got tough, his direction was clear—stand taller, work harder, and be more creative. He once explained to me that his leadership style is to hire talented people, ask for a little more than seems possible or realistic, and then demand results. No excuses. Ron set the bar high, and because I hate to underachieve and admired my boss a great deal, I worked hard not to let him down.

It didn't take long to discover my boss had a casual manner and little patience for protocol, formalities, or hierarchy. On one occasion, I was working on a politically sensitive op-ed, and he wanted a second opinion on some of the language. He instructed me to call Israel's newly appointed ambassador in Washington and ask his opinion on a few of the points. Israelis are casual by nature, but this seemed like a particularly acute breach of protocol.

I relayed his instructions to Dafna and asked, "So, how does it work? Do you coordinate a time with the ambassador's assistant?"

Dafna gave me one of her trademark withering looks, "No."

She scribbled something on a sticky note and handed it to me, "This is his cell phone number, call him."

Taken aback, I looked at the number and stuttered, "But he won't know who I am."

"Then tell him your name." And with that she waved me off.

I walked slowly to my office and gingerly placed the paper with the phone number on my desk. OK, I thought. No big deal. I'll just go ahead and call Israel's ambassador to the United States on his cell phone. He's probably busy meeting the president and won't answer anyway.

I dialed the ambassador's number, and he answered on the second ring. Trying to keep the nervousness out of my voice, I explained who I was and why I was calling. Finding nothing about the situation at all unusual, he answered my questions about the op-ed and then asked, "How's it going over there? Has anyone pushed you out a window yet?"

Caught off guard, I answered a little too quickly, "I didn't know that was something I had to worry about. I assumed I should be more concerned about the drones."

"Nah," he answered, "he pushes you out a window and we have the drones get you on the way down, just to be sure the job is done."

I laughed. Nervously.

We wrapped up the call, and I shook my head as I placed the phone back on its receiver. File that under conversations I never had working for Canadians.

———

While there was never any doubt Ron was the final authority at the Mission, he encouraged his staff to challenge his opinions. This came easily to the Israelis, but for many of the non-Israeli interns, this took some getting used to. They would sit quietly listening to us discuss an upcoming debate or something in the news, and Ron would abruptly turn to one of them and say, "Don't just sit there, what do you think?"

Caught off guard, the intern would stutter and try to formulate an answer.

Ron would declare, 'I can't hear you, speak up."

A moment later he would say to the flame-faced intern, "I always do that. You'll get used to it." And sure enough, they did. As time passed, the interns became bolder and would offer their opinions without being asked.

Ron loved a good debate, but it wasn't easy to change his mind when he had settled on an idea or a plan. On one occasion, I was working on a speech that would be delivered to a women's group, and Ron instructed me to write that in the entire Arab world, there isn't a single female leader.

I interjected, "It's not true."

"Of course, it's true." He continued, "Name one female leader in the Arab world."

"I'll name two." I answered, "Queen Noor and Queen Rania of Jordan. Both are highly respected and involved in global education initiatives."

"They don't count," Ron replied, "Neither of them was elected."

"Neither were you," I shot back, "That doesn't mean you aren't an effective leader."

Ron laughed and with a characteristic waggle of his finger, he pointed at me and said, "Aviva Klompas, you may be a little right, but on the larger point, you are still wrong."

———

It took months and hundreds of drafts for me to learn to write in the unique style of Ron Prosor. I knew I had finally grown into my job when I stopped feeling a cold terror in UN sessions when Ron would slip me a note instructing me to write a witty retort in response to something a delegate had just said. I usually had about two minutes to come up with a one-liner that would pass muster.

The ink is barely dry on the interim nuclear agreement and Iran is already showing its true colors. This is a regime that crosses red lines, produces yellow cake, and beats its citizens black and blue.

[SPEECH TO THE SECURITY COUNCIL,
JANUARY 2014]

In Saudi Arabia, women need a guardian's permission to marry, take classes and travel. It is also the only country in the world that bans women from driving a car. Not long ago, a few brave women defied the ban and were detained by police and fined for the so-called crime of tarnishing the Kingdom's reputation. Tarnishing the Kingdom's reputation? The real stain on the Kingdom is its failure to recognize that by relegating half of its population to the backseat, Saudi Arabia is being steered off course.

[SPEECH TO SECOND COMMITTEE,
FEBRUARY 2014]

Rather than working productively to advance sustainable development, some delegations have exploited this professional and focused debate to further a political agenda that singles out Israel. The World Cup may be taking place in Rio, but it seems a world coup is taking place in these halls. This forum is being used as a stadium to take cheap shots at Israel.

[HIGH-LEVEL POLITICAL FORUM ON
SUSTAINABLE DEVELOPMENT, JULY 2014]

Every nation that voted in favor of the Palestinian's one-sided resolution encouraged them to continue their diplomatic triathlon—running away from negotiations, placing hurdles into the peace process, and cycling towards protracted conflict.

[SPEECH TO SECOND COMMITTEE, JANUARY 2015]

I had also come to see how Ron's signature style was effective. Most speeches delivered in the United Nations are technical and dull. Few delegations employ a locally-based speechwriter, so remarks get written by a subject matter expert who may or may not be fluent in English. Ron was adamant he would never be accused of the ultimate crime: being boring. He wanted people to listen and he was willing to push the limits of diplomacy in the process. Frequently, he reminded me of Winston Churchill's famous quip, "Diplomacy is the art of telling people to go to hell in such a way that they ask for directions."

In Israel, Ron often made headlines for his caustic barbs that exposed the hypocrisy of the world body. These same taunts made him something of a celebrity at the United Nations. His fellow ambassadors would stop him in the corridors and quote a line from a speech or chuckle that his were the only memorable speeches. Of course, there were many diplomats, and even some of my colleagues, who would have liked to see him tone it down or behave in a more conventional manner, but the last thing Ron aspired to was being conventional. To be sure, he was playing to the crowds, but he also genuinely believed that if he could get more people to listen to his speeches, he could make at least some of them better understand Israel's point of view.

This also explains why Ron was always pestering me to come up with metaphors to convey a point he wanted to make. If he felt something I had written was complex or convoluted, he would remind me that most countries are largely uninterested in Israel's hyper-political situation. The purpose of every speech was to ensure the listener gained a new insight into the complex challenges faced by the Jewish state and not slip into a semi-conscious state, lost in convoluted legalese digressions.

———————

Once I understood Ron's thinking, we fell into a comfortable partnership and started producing speeches that captured attention. It was particularly rewarding when other Missions would call asking for a copy of our latest speech, as was the case with a speech to the General Assembly on The New Partnership for Africa's Development (NEPAD).

I wrote the speech with help from Simonne, our Second Committee Representative. A fellow Canadian and the epitome of kindness, Simonne was always willing to help edit, think through a problem, or listen to me gripe. Together, we wrote a speech that outlined the many challenges the nations of Africa had already overcome and addressed ways in which cooperation and innovation could bring greater stability and prosperity to the continent. Together, we took the speech to Ron. He read it aloud and when he was finished said, "I like it." Simonne and I smiled at one another. He continued, "But you're missing something." Our smiles froze, we waited nervously. "You need to add in Shakira."

I had no idea what he was talking about.

"Err, Ron. Shakira is from Latin America."

"Aviva-leh," Ron said, "It is clear to me that you do not really know Shakira."

I couldn't argue.

He continued, "She has a song about Africa, *Waka Waka Africa*. Put in a few lines." He started to hum a few bars from the song, which sounded familiar.

Simonne and I found the lyrics to the song and were pleased to see they would easily fit into the speech. A few days later, Ron rose to the podium of the General Assembly to deliver the speech. Simonne and I sat at Israel's table and listened. As Ron approached the end of his speech, we waited to see if he would indeed sing as he had half-promised, half-threatened to do on the walk over to the General Assembly. As Ron reached the final lines of his speech he said:

There is an African proverb that says, "If you want to go quickly, go alone. If you want to go far, go together." This is what NEPAD is about—Africans forging Africa's future, together.

A new wave of optimism is sweeping through the plains, mountains and savannahs of Africa. But in order for this optimism to take hold, every child and every family and every community must have the opportunity to build a brighter future.

So let us pledge to empower the people of Africa. Let us commit to ensuring they have equal opportunities. And let us strive to ensure a brighter future for all of Africa's people.

As musical superstar Shakira says in her song, "This Time for Africa":
Today's your day
I feel it
You paved the way
Believe it . . .
This time for Africa!

Thank you, Madam President.

[SPEECH TO THE GENERAL ASSEMBLY, OCTOBER 2013]

True to his word, Ron sang the last line, "This time for Africa!" As he stepped off the podium, the room erupted in applause, a practice unheard of in General Assembly sessions. Delegates from African nations rose to their feet and walked to the front of the room to hug and congratulate Ron. The president of the General Assembly leaned into her microphone and said, "I thank the delegate from Israel." She paused and continued, "I like that song also."

———————

With that, the singing diplomat was born. In a debate on population development, Ron spoke about the need to invest in and support women, children, and civil society, and concluded by singing a few lines from John Lennon's "Imagine."

In a speech to the Commission on Population and Development, Ron asked me to write about empowering women. I immediately knew the song to include in the speech and working with Simonne, wrote the following:

Mr. Chairman,

The Queen of Soul, Aretha Franklin, sang: "R-E-S-P-E-C-T. Find out what it means to me!"

This song is an anthem for anyone who has ever felt marginalized or minimized. Every human being craves respect—the opportunity to earn a decent living, raise his family, and contribute to his community.

[SPEECH TO THE COMMISSION ON
POPULATION AND DEVELOPMENT, APRIL 2015]

When a speech included a song, I could expect Ron to belt out the tune in the car on the short drive to the UN complex. Some colleagues voiced their opposition to including songs in speeches, arguing it made light of serious issues. Ron believed just the opposite. He felt it brought attention to important topics by giving people something to talk about.

There were only a couple of intances when I included lyrics in the more somber Security Council. Ron never sang in the Council, but he used the lyrics to convey his message. When Arik Einstein, one of Israel's most popular singer/songwriters, passed away, he eulogized him by concluding his speech with words from his most famous song, "Ani Veata" (Me and You):

> *You and I will change the world*
> *You and I, and others will join us*
> *They have said it before*
> *It doesn't matter, because you and I will change the world.*
>
> [SPEECH TO THE SECURITY COUNCIL,
> NOVEMBER 2013]

In another Security Council debate, Ron used Leonard Cohen's song "Democracy," to make the point the Arab Spring would not bring about democracy, saying, "It's coming from the feel that this ain't exactly real, or it's real, but it ain't exactly there."

The inclusion of Leonard Cohen was Ron's idea. I was against it for a purely pragmatic reason. He could not properly pronounce Leonard. No matter how much we practiced, it always came out sounding like Leo-nard. Ron's English is excellent, but there were a handful of words that just didn't sound right when he read them. King Solomon, sounded like King Sal-a-mon, Nobel Laureate was always Nobel Lah-ter-at, and Secretariat came out in an undistinguishable jumble of sounds.

Prior to delivery, Ron read every speech back to me out loud, so we could hear if the rhythm or pronunciations were problematic. If a word didn't sound right, I offered a synonym. It didn't happen often, but from time to time Ron stumbled over his words during his delivery, and the sentence came out with an unexpected meaning. In a speech to entrepreneurs Ron was supposed to say,

You come from many nations and speak many languages. But today you have converged to form a global tapestry of imagination woven by common threads.

In his delivery, however, he said, "Together, you form a global *pastry* of imagination." I wondered what the delegates listening in Chinese or Spanish or Arabic made of that line.

Sometimes the pronunciation errors amounted to minor diplomatic gaffes. On one occasion Ron was asked to deliver remarks at an event recognizing the steadfast support of the Canadian government. Canada's foreign minister at the time, John Baird (pronounced Beh-rd), would be there to represent the Canadian government. When we practiced the speech, Ron kept pronouncing the Foreign minister's name as John *Bird*. I would correct him, but in the next read through he would go back to John Bird. Before we stepped out of the car to go into the event, I offered, "Ron, you can remember the correct pronunciation using this rhyme 'If only everyone cared as much as John Baird.' Dafna and I escorted Ron into the venue and, as was our habit, made our way to the bar. When the time came, Ron stepped to the podium and declared, "It's a pleasure to be here to recognize John Bird." I turned to Dafna and groaned. She clinked my glass with her own and said, "Drink up, dear. It's all you can do now." I needn't have worried. His warmth and geniality came across in his speeches and earned him great applause.

Ron had a wicked sense of humor, and sometimes used these mispronunciations to his advantage. On July 22, 2013, Prince William and his wife Catherine, duke and duchess of Cambridge, announced the birth of their son, Prince George. That evening, I was in my office working on a Situation in the Middle East speech that would be delivered the following morning. As with all the Middle East speeches, it had been weeks of long days and lots of edits. My phone rang.

"Hello?" I answered, still typing.

Ron was on the line, "Aviva, I have an addition for the speech."

Good grief, I thought. I had only just started his last round of edits.

Ron continued, "At the beginning of the speech, I would like you to add this: On a personal note, I would like to congratulate the British Ambassador, Sir Mark Lyall Grant, and the British people on the birth of a new heir."

He pronounced heir as *hair*. I hesitated, wondering whether to correct his pronunciation, but before I could answer, Ron continued, "Then finish with God *shave* the queen."

I was silent as I tried to figure out if he was serious. After a long pause, I heard Dafna snicker in the background. Then the two of them burst into hysterical laughter, before hanging up. Fabulous. I was being prank called by my boss.

———————

To be sure, my time working for Israel at the United Nations was difficult and draining, but it was also deeply satisfying and quite a lot of fun. There were karaoke evenings, pumpkin carving contests, office pranks, a toy air cannon that shot soft foam balls, outings with the interns to the Bryant Park skating rink, and plenty of open bar receptions.

One evening, a few of us left the office early to enjoy drinks at a nearby rooftop bar. Dafna and I were only going to stay a short while before walking to the United Nations to meet Ron and escort him to an event. I had a little more to drink than I should have and was tipsy by the time we rose and hastily said goodbye to our colleagues. As we walked the few blocks over to the United Nations, I swayed a little and laughed just a bit too loudly. We arrived and stood in the semicircle driveway in front of the Secretariat building waiting for Ron to pull up.

Unaffected by her drinks, Dafna turned to me with a serious look and said, "Now pull it together."

I nodded soberly and stifled a giggle.

"Really, darling," she said, "you need to keep it together."

Ron's black car pulled up just then. He climbed out of the car and made a beeline toward me. Something I had done—I can't recall what—had irritated him and he started to lecture me. Eyes flickering toward Dafna, I stared straight ahead and did my best to somberly and slowly nod. From the way Dafna was looking at me, I imagine I looked more like one of those dunking birds in a top hat—the contraption with two glass bulbs joined by a glass tube—that bobs up and down. Dafna took in the scene and stepped in to usher Ron inside and upstairs to the reception. When he was seated, she found me at the back of the room and asked, "Shall we get a drink?"

———————

There were times when my workplace seemed completely unreasonable. On more than one occasion, I handed Ron a speech draft to read and he demanded to know why he had agreed to give the speech in the first place. He knew perfectly well I had nothing to do with the scheduling of his speaking engagements. Once, when an event was scheduled to take place in his home, he called to ask me if there was a podium in his living room. I was tempted to suggest he peer around the corner and see if there was a podium set up between his sofas, but instead said I'd call Dafna to check. I also vividly recall the time he gathered a few staff together and ordered us to find a Jon Stewart clip he had seen the night before and wanted to send to a friend. A couple of interns got to work and sent Ron two options based on the very vague description he had given us. Neither was the clip Ron had in mind, so they tried again. Still wrong. This went on for a couple of days, with Ron growing increasingly annoyed with each failed effort to locate the mysterious Jon Stewart clip. The mystery was finally solved when, after further questioning and much internet scouring, we discovered Ron had been watching Bill Maher.

Ron's saving grace was his quick wit. He was a great admirer of Shimon Peres and could imitate the late Israeli prime minister and president with uncanny accuracy. There were countless times, when we were sitting discussing a speech or a letter, when Ron would slip into his Peres voice and reel off a favorite saying such as, "The Jews' greatest contribution to history is dissatisfaction. We're a nation born to be discontented. Whatever exists we believe can be changed for the better."

Once he got started, he would keep reciting Peres's favorite expressions, "In our river flows more history than water," or "We will take the salt out of the sea and the hatred out of their hearts," or "We used to be the people of the book, now we became the people of the Facebook."

When President Peres visited New York, Ron invited me along to meet the iconic head of state. There were only a handful of people in the room and, as we entered, I heard President Peres speaking. I turned to Ron amazed he would do his impersonation in front of the president. It took me a moment to realize I was hearing the real Shimon Peres speaking. Ron's impersonation was spot on.

The Jewish people have given the world the comedy of Jerry Seinfeld, Joan Rivers, Jackie Mason, Jon Stewart, and Sarah Silverman, but when it comes to Israel, we quickly lose our sense of humor. Not Ron. One of the first decisions he made when he was appointed Israel's ambassador to the United Nations was that the entire delegation needed to lighten up. He instructed the diplomats to more frequently exercise a rule of procedure known as a right of reply. It is a rebuttal that is invoked when a delegate feels his or her personal or national integrity has been publicly insulted. Israel's integrity was insulted on an almost daily basis at the United Nations, but until Ron arrived, rights of reply were sparingly employed. Under Ron's ambassadorship, we employed them with regularity, and I was frequently called upon to write them.

I'm glad to hear the delegate from Iran is citing an example of Israel's free and open press. Perhaps if there was a similar free and open press under his own government, I could read a similar article from an Iranian newspaper that questioned the policies of his own government.

Earlier, the Syrian delegate launched a series of baseless accusations against Israel. I suppose we should be glad he is launching words instead of the rockets that his government routinely launches at its citizens.

During quieter periods, I would challenge myself to write themed rights of reply. During the February 2014 Sochi Olympics, I came up with:

Millions of people may have turned their attention to the Sochi Olympics, but right here at the U.N. you can find delegates who are skating on thin ice and performing unbelievable rhetorical feats.

The week before the Oscars, we used:

> *This weekend, Hollywood will distribute Academy Awards to top performers in the entertainment industry. I am considering nominating some of the delegates who spoke in this Chamber earlier—they have become experts at scripting fiction, delivering lines, and producing the world's worst humanitarian crisis.*

As winter turned to spring we used:

> *Outside the thaw of a long winter is lifting, but here in the United Nations, Israel continues to receive a chilly reception from certain delegates. Faced with a storm of icy accusations, Israel has no choice but to reply.*

CHAPTER 6

Ma ani, ez? / What am I, a goat?

Who's calling the shots?

Before I started working at the Israeli Mission, a friend put me in touch with Gregory Levey, the author of a tongue-in-cheek memoir about his own time working as a speechwriter for the Israeli government. I had read the book a few years earlier when I was interning at the Israeli Consulate in New York and marveled at how much Greg and I had in common. We are both Canadians who moved from Toronto to New York for graduate school. We both held internships for the Israelis and, through unlikely circumstances, both became speechwriters at the Israeli Mission. Greg had been speechwriter for Dan Gillerman, Israel's thirteenth ambassador to the United Nations. After a year at the Mission, Greg was transferred to Jerusalem to write English speeches for Prime Minister Ariel Sharon.

Around the office, Greg was spoken about in hushed whispers and described as, "the guy who wrote the book." I always found it odd that there were half a dozen copies of his book scattered around the office. It occasionally worked in my favor. We had a new diplomat start at the Mission and when he learned I was the Mission speechwriter, he asked if I was planning to write a book. He repeated the question from time to time as the months passed. I laughed off the question or brushed aside the inquiry, but once or twice, when I didn't fully agree with a position he wanted written in a letter or speech, I would jokingly ask, "Are you sure? This could end up in my book." It was enough to get him to think twice.

I called Greg before starting my speechwriting position, and he offered useful suggestions. He advised that summers were the slower time of year, and I should use those months to prepare for the chaos of the Fall General Assembly. For four months, from September to December, the United Nations is at its busiest and Israel sends extra diplomats to represent the Jewish state. In addition to writing speeches for Ron, I would need to have speeches ready for diplomats representing the United Nations' six committees.

As we approached the summer months, I drew up a list of the dozens of speeches that would be needed in the fall. Many would be written by specialists in Israel, but both Greg and Nate had warned me it took far more time to correct the mangled English than to simply write it myself. I reviewed the list of speeches: they covered topics as diverse as Sports for Peace and Development, Conflict Diamonds, and Global Road Safety. I set a goal of getting all the GA speeches done by the end of August, mapped out a plan on my whiteboard, and got to work.

———————

As summer came to an end, it came time to say goodbye to Avishai, who was leaving the Mission to pursue a career in law. I had dreaded the day, but now it was time to bid adieu to my friend, confidant, and writing partner. We threw him a rooftop party in Brooklyn. It was a bittersweet gathering. When the time came, we gathered together to toast our friend. To thank him for spending months patiently teaching me Ron's unique brand of humor, I wrote a speech that described the classic six-step process of writing for Ron Prosor.

Step one: *play with the name. Avishai Don—You weren't shy when you donned the cap of speechwriter.*

Step two: *tell a joke at the U.N.'s expense. Avishai—your experience with us will prove to be a good foundation for a legal career—after all, much of what goes on at the U.N. is nothing short of criminal.*

Step three: *liberal use of metaphors. Avishai, there have been stormy seas, but you have been the lighthouse shining the way to calmer waters.*

Step four: *add Churchill. "Never, never, never give up."*

Step five: *insert questionably funny sound bite. The Israeli Mission without Avishai is like the Mafia without its best assassin—we need him for our jokes to hit the mark.*

Step six: *finish off with rousing conclusion. Avishai—you saved me on numerous occasions and I expect you'll save me on many more—don't change your email address.*

Avishai had also prepared a speech. He shared a few favorite stories before turning to me and saying, "I was there to train a hapless, innocent Canadian in a field in which I had since become an expert: the fine art of writing like a diplomatic son-of-a-bitch . . . Ron—it doesn't take the detective skills of Sherlock Holmes to deduce that you can be a difficult man to write for."

True on both counts.

On his last day in the office, Avishai handed me a gift. Inside was a compass. I laughed as I picked it up and examined the inscription. Ron had taken to spotting me and proclaiming in his deep, booming voice, "Aviva Klompas, do you have your moral compass??"

Inscribed on the brass gift was: "Aviva Klompas, use this compass to help you navigate the U.N.'s stormy seas. Best, Avishai."

———————

After Avishai departed, I set about bolstering the speechwriting ranks. Knowing my workload would skyrocket during the General Assembly, I was keen to hire two interns. Some of my colleagues argued it wasn't necessary for me to have two interns, but I wasn't taking no for an answer. I finally landed on an argument they couldn't disagree with: we didn't pay our interns, so why not hire two?

After weeks poring through résumés, I narrowed the prospects to a handful of promising candidates and passed their names to the colleague responsible for hiring interns. I let him know I planned to give them all a writing assignment, so I could shortlist candidates to interview.

"Why?" he asked.

Sensing I was about to get sucked into an Israeli HR black hole, I cautiously answered, "To find out if they can write speeches."

"But they gave you a writing sample already. They submitted it with their application."

"True, but most of them gave me academic papers. I want to give them one hour to write soundbites for Ron. It'll be a much better assessment of their speechwriting abilities."

"That seems unfair to me."

"How can that possibly be unfair?" I asked incredulously.

"They are unpaid interns. We cannot ask them to do something that will cause so much pressure."

I was bewildered. "You're kidding, right?"

"Of course not," he responded.

This debate continued for days. I argued that if they could not handle writing five-minute snatches in an hour, they'd be no use to us. If this assignment overwhelmed them, I contended, they would have a heart attack from the daily stress in our office.

The intern overlord finally relented, and I sent out the writing assignments. I picked out the few I wanted to interview, and was surprised to learn our elections officer, chief of staff, the deputy ambassador, and his assistant all intended to participate in the interview.

I went to find Ella and asked, "You don't think it's overkill to have five staff interview an intern?"

"No," she replied.

"You really don't think it's a colossal, total waste of time for the deputy ambassador and chief of staff to be part of the process?" I continued.

"It shows how seriously we take the position," Ella replied.

Or how absurd our hiring practices are, I thought, as I resigned myself to the situation.

After selecting the interns I wanted to hire, the Mission began the long and tedious security clearance process. It took so long that I frequently lost good candidates who declined to wait out the process and accepted another internship offer instead.

In one interview a candidate asked me how long the security clearance would take. I smiled and answered, "That depends. Are you a terrorist?" We all had a good laugh and then wrapped up his interview. A few weeks later, I was told the candidate did not pass his clearance. It was futile to ask why because the security team would never share the details. I found Keinan, the Mission's election officer who also helped with the hiring of interns, and passed along the news. "I guess he was a terrorist." I told him. "It's a pity. He was a pretty good writer for a terrorist."

We selected two Australian candidates to assist me with speechwriting for the fall, Nathan and Raphael. They were both law students who opted to spend a few months working for the Israeli Mission before returning to school in Nathan's case, or starting his career in Raphael's case. Funny, eloquent, and stylish dressers, Nathan and Raphael made the torturous months of the General Assembly fun. It didn't take long for them to pick up Ron's style of wit and begin to write some outstandingly scathing lines. They competed with one another to see whose work would impress Ron more, and more importantly, whose work would be derided. When Ron thought a speech was boring or pedantic, he would toss the papers across his table and declare the speech "shite." Raphael made a chart to hang in the intern room and keep track of who got the most shites from Ron. Much to the Australians' dismay, I never made their shite list. They didn't need to know I had earned more than my fair share of shite feedback in my first few months on the job.

On occasion, Raphael and Nathan would hand me drafts of letters or speeches and I'd find them peppered with unfamiliar expressions. Their conversations included words like arvo, go troppo, ripper, and sickie. They were surprised to discover these favorite phrases were unheard-of in North America. Sometimes, this cultural gap led to unexpected surprises. Once, when we were asked to prepare a birthday greeting for Ron to send to fellow ambassadors, Raphael volunteered for the assignment. He sent me an email with the following suggestion:

Winston Churchill once said, "We are happier in many ways when we are old than when we were young. The young sow wild oats. The old grow sage."

It gives me great pleasure to congratulate you on your birthday and express my hope that you remain fit enough to sow oats, as you continue in happiness to grow sage.

I grabbed the phone and called Raphael in the intern office.

"Hey Raph, swing by my office," I paused and continued, "and bring your iPhone." He arrived a minute later.

"Raph—do me a favor. Google 'sow wild oats' on your phone."

With a curious look, he began typing and I watched as the realization dawned on him. He read aloud, "If a young man sows his wild oats, he has a period of his life when he has a lot of exciting sexual relationships." Raphael started to giggle.

I smiled at him and said, "It may not be the best phrase to include in a birthday greeting to an ambassador."

"Right! Back to the drawing board," Raphael cheerfully replied and turned to leave my office, still snickering.

New York is an expensive city. I could only afford to live in Manhattan because I worked constantly and never had time for shopping or leisure activities. I wasn't the only one being paid meagerly. Everyone at the Mission was in the same difficult position. In March of 2014, staff in Israel's Foreign Ministry declared a general strike. The strike came after nearly two years of negotiations between the union representing diplomats and Israel's Ministry of Finance for improved salaries and working conditions. One hundred and three Israeli missions were shuttered around the world along with the Foreign Ministry's headquarters in Jerusalem.

For the first time since moving to New York, I had free time on my hands. There was a great deal of speculation and confusion about the strike. It wasn't clear if it would last one day or one month and rumors flew that we wouldn't be paid for the duration. Even if we were paid, the overtime hours I depended on were obviously off the table.

There was little to do but wait and see. Simonne and I called Ron and asked if he wanted to meet for lunch. He readily agreed, and we met at a deli in midtown. As we sat down and looked over the menu, Ron called over the waiter, pointed to his security detail, and said, "Ask them what they want and add it to my bill." Over lunch, Ron regaled us with stories from his diplomatic postings in Bonn and Washington. Simonne and I told him about our previous jobs and where we hoped our respective careers would eventually take us.

Ten days after the strike began, Foreign Ministry workers signed an agreement with Finance Ministry officials to increase pay for Israeli diplomats, bringing the strike to an end and sending all of us back to work. Months later, I asked one of the diplomats if they received their pay increases. He laughed and told me that not only had they not seen a pay raise, their salaries were docked for every day they were on strike.

Incredulous, I asked, "But then what did the strike achieve?"

"Beats me," he answered.

As soon as the strike ended, we returned to work with a vengeance. I had bid farewell to Nathan and Rafael a couple months earlier, and their positions had yet to be filled with new interns. Most days, I returned home from work and fell exhausted onto my couch. The workload piled up unrelentingly. In addition to being sorely understaffed, time management skills seemed to run counterculture to some of my colleagues. After a harrowing couple of months, I was determined to have a strong speechwriting intern with me over the summer. It was difficult to attract talent given the stringent HR parameters. Many students were interested in the position but balked at the prospect of living in New York City without a salary. On top of that, the Mission's bureaucracy moved glacially slowly and refused to give any indication to a prospective candidate if he or she would be accepted until they had been checked by security—and that took months.

One afternoon in April, I was in my office putting the finishing touches on a General Assembly speech for the following morning. I had a huge backlog of assignments and was desperately behind on writing a major Security Council speech. Noa rushed into my office to tell me she had to give a statement tomorrow and asked if I would look at what she had written.

I looked up from my monitor, scowled, and asked, "You just found out now you have to give a statement tomorrow?"

"Not exactly," came the sheepish reply.

"You'll have to get an intern to look at it for you," I said with a sigh and turned back to my computer monitor.

She came around to my side of the desk and pleaded, "There are no writing interns—please, it's not very long, just four or five pages."

Impatiently I snapped, "There are native English-speaking interns. They can do the first round of edits and then I'll look at it."

Noa was persistent, "I can't trust them to edit it. Come on. You could do it quickly. It doesn't even have to be perfect."

Just then, Anat, the Mission's new spokesperson, came into my office and announced, "I think I can get us more media coverage for tomorrow's speech if you just change a few things."

My stomach clenched. "Just change a few things?" I asked.

She started to outline the changes she wanted to make, and I grew agitated as she explained she wanted to insert some dry facts and figures in place of a section I had spent a long time carefully crafting.

Keinan walked into my office, oblivious to the scene around him, and declared, "Bad news. I don't think that your summer intern candidate is willing to wait for us to get him cleared by security."

"Can you blame him?" I exploded. "We've kept him waiting for weeks and he has another offer from a normal office with reasonable colleagues," I continued, utterly exasperated. "Why can't security meet with him this week?" I demanded.

"Because it's already this week," he replied seriously.

"It's Monday," I sputtered. "There are four more days in this week. We could devote an hour or two to meeting this candidate, so I can have some help. I need help. Not in a month, not in two weeks. Today, right now!"

"It seems unlikely," he replied calmly and turned to leave my office.

Fully worked up, I stood and turned to Noa and Anat, "Did it occur to either of you that I might have other plans this evening? Do you really think I should sit here all day and night to be at the beck and call of every person in this office?"

Unfazed by my bad temper, they both looked at me expectantly. I was no match for the two Israelis. I sighed and sank into my seat to look at Noa's speech.

In addition to dealing with the demanding work culture in the Mission, I had to navigate complicated internal politics. Everybody had an agenda—someone to answer to in Israel, a UN counterpart to impress, an issue to sensationalize, or a grudge to pursue. The competing interests could be particularly noticeable when we responded to UN reports. Some colleagues wanted me to quote entire sections verbatim in speeches or letters. Doing so was akin to giving an approving nod to the country or UN official that authored the report. In most cases, I knew the combination of technical jargon and tired UN language would never pass muster with Ron, so I would take the spirit and sentiment of the text and fashion it into language that would resonate.

For example, a report on Commission and Population Development said, "Recognizing that poverty is both the cause and the result of social exclusion and that quality education is a path to individual agency, both income inequality and education gains since Cairo are addressed in this chapter."

Substantively important, but no chance Ron would agree to read something so technical, so I wrote: "When a girl is deprived of an education, poverty is passed to the next generation. When a young entrepreneur can't start a new business, a nation's economy stagnates. And when a woman is denied equal rights, the shadow of repression looms large."

Just when I'd cleared the hurdles of internal politics, I could learn the Arab nations had rallied to undermine Israel. A day before Ron was scheduled to deliver a speech to the Commission on Population and Development, the G77 issued a statement haranguing Israel. The Group of 77, or G77, is a coalition of developing nations working to promote its members' collective economic interests. There were seventy-seven founding member states, but by 2013 the organization had 133 members. I suppose nobody thought to update the name of the group. At the behest of some Arab states, Bolivia delivered a statement on behalf of the G77:

The Group of 77 and China calls upon the international community to give priority attention to the plight of people living under foreign occupation, forced displacement, and armed conflict, and put an end to their suffering, including by removing obstacles facing the development of their health system, by ensuring protection of their human rights, access to health care and services, education and development and by enhancing technical and financial assistance; in particular for the people of the occupied State of Palestine, who continue to be victims of forced displacement, home demolitions, and land confiscations for the construction of illegal settlement and the annexation Wall.

"Foreign occupation" was a buzzword that sent members of the Israeli delegation into a tizzy. There are a number of countries in the world with border disputes. China has Tibet, India and Pakistan have Kashmir, Turkey has Northern Cyprus, and Morocco has the Western Sahara. But when a member state at the United Nations says "foreign occupation," they are always referring to Israel. Bolivia's statement set off a heated debate in the office as to whether we should respond, and, if so, what to say. After twenty-four hours of back and forth, the diplomats settled on a vague and mild allusion to the G77 statement in our prepared remarks:

> *Imagine if governments were truly committed to bettering the lives of their citizens. Yesterday, the very nations that prohibit women from driving, from getting an education, and from voting had the audacity to accuse Israel—the only democracy in the Middle East. Instead of helping people realize their dreams, these nations have trapped their people in a nightmare.*

To paraphrase Ron, it would take the likes of Sherlock Holmes to see how those three sentences served to answer the accusations. Nonetheless, my colleagues were mollified and often that was victory enough.

There were times when I tried hard to keep politics out of a speech, as was the case when Israel organized an art exhibit called Speaking Colors. The exhibition coincided with the first day of a conference on the Convention on the Rights of Persons with Disabilities. The session had a special focus on youth with disabilities, and the main floor of UN Headquarters was dotted with paintings made by Israeli children with autism.

On opening night, UN Secretary-General Ban Ki-moon and Ron were scheduled to deliver remarks. Noa was the lead staff member for this event and together we prepared Ron's remarks. The day of the event also happened to be the day Reuven Rivlin was elected Israel's tenth president. A couple of hours before the event, Anat, our spokesperson, came into my office and said she could get us a lot of media attention if Ron adjusted his speech a bit.

I narrowed my eyes. "What do you mean 'adjusted'?'"

Undeterred by my withering glare, she continued, "I think we should congratulate Rivlin and then say the Arabs could learn from us about holding elections."

Confused, I asked, "Why on earth would I say such a thing in a speech about Israel's contributions to disability rights? This is a nice, non-political event. This is Israel being a normal country and not just a conflict."

"But it's not sexy. We won't get any media coverage," she pressed.

"That may well be, but it's not always about getting good press."

"I disagree." She stood before me arms crossed and determined.

Seeing we were at an impasse, I texted Noa to let her know what was being proposed.

The reply came back almost instantly: "Over my dead body."

I showed Noa's answer to Anat and she said, "Listen. It's my job to get Ron press and my suggestion will get Ron press."

I answered, "It's also *our* job to represent Israel. Dragging politics into an event celebrating the artwork of autistic children is a mistake."

We continued arguing. I had yet to fully internalize the futility of arguing with Israelis. They rarely relent. Just then Ella came into my office and, hearing us quarrel, suggested a compromise of sorts: "How about, we congratulate Rivlin and then invite him to come to the U.N. to see the great work we are doing."

"I can live with that," I offered.

Seeing it was the best she would get, Anat grudgingly agreed and left to write a press release.

I turned to Ella, "Good thing you did that conflict resolution course. It comes in handy around here." She smiled in the doorway of my office and said, "I should have done a children's development course instead. It would have made it easier to work with all you people."

Ella was always good at putting us in our place.

CHAPTER 7

Balagan / A mess

What's the protocol when your intern gets arrested?

As fall approached, the office began preparing for the new session of
the General Assembly. The second week of the session is known as
high-level week. Heads of state and foreign ministers descend on
New York to attend the general debate. The period is notorious in New York
for midtown gridlock created by vast numbers of motorcades and road
blocks.

Each country is allotted fifteen minutes to address the General Assembly,
though many speakers see this as a vague suggestion rather than a guideline.
The longest speech on record was given in 1960 by Cuban president Fidel
Castro and it lasted 269 minutes. In 2009, Libya's Muammar Qaddafi spent
ninety-six minutes delivering an eccentric rant against the UN Security
Council.

Like all major sessions, the speeches are translated into the UN official
languages: Arabic, Chinese, English, French, Russian, and Spanish. A curious tradition dictates that Brazil's head of state speaks first even though it is
neither the host nation nor first alphabetically. The reason is that in the early
years of the United Nations, countries were reluctant to speak first, but
Brazil volunteered and thus earned the right to do so ever since.

In the leadup to the opening session of the General Assembly, there were two great debates in our office. Iran had just elected a new president, Hassan Rouhani, and a decision had to be made as to whether our ambassador would sit in the General Assembly while the Iranian leader delivered remarks. For eight successive years, Mahmoud Ahmadinejad had attended high-level week and devoted his time at the podium spouting paranoid theories, spewing reprehensible slurs against Israel, and denying the Holocaust. Jerusalem had instructed its delegates to walk out rather than hear Ahmadinejad speak. President Rouhani had barely been in office a month, but the media and international community had already celebrated him as the darling new "moderate" of Iran. Israelis were understandingly skeptical.

The second debate in our office was over which Cabinet minister would be sent to represent Israel. Prime Minister Netanyahu would arrive towards the end of the month to deliver remarks to the General Assembly, but a minister would need to arrive earlier to represent Israel in a marathon of meetings. It seemed to swing between two options, minister of justice or minister of intelligence, international relations, and strategic affairs.

Ultimately it was decided that the latter would attend and deliver three speeches. I was told his speeches would be drafted in Israel, but I might be called upon to make last minute edits. I had fallen for this before. When previous delegates had come from Israel, I had similarly been reassured they would arrive with speeches in hand, only to have them land in New York and look to me expectantly. I prepared three speeches for the minister. A few days before he arrived, I was told there had been a change in plans and I was to write his speeches and send them to Jerusalem for review.

Early Monday morning of high-level week, I was at home eating breakfast when Ella called. "We need you at the hotel." Never one to parse words, she continued, "I'm texting you the address, come as quickly as you can and bring copies of the minister's speeches." I rushed out the door and caught the train to Grand Central Station. I exited into the early morning sunshine and

jogged the few blocks to the hotel. Traffic was heavily congested. Police officers were stationed on nearly every corner. In front of the hotel, barricades
were set up and guests were being ushered through a metal detector. As I
stepped into the ornate lobby, I saw Ron, Ella, Dafna, and Keinan sitting on
a couch, calmly sipping cups of Starbucks Coffee.

"What's going on?" I asked as I walked up to them.

Ella answered, "The minister is on his way over."

"OK," I replied, sitting down in one of the plush chairs, "what happens
when he arrives?"

"Gerber wants to go over the speeches with you," Ron answered.

I would have continued asking questions about who Gerber was and what
I needed to do, but they had already picked up the conversation I had interrupted. I sank back in my chair and watched the parade of well-dressed
diplomats saunter around the lobby under rows of sparkling chandeliers.
Thirty minutes later, the Israeli delegation arrived.

Ron introduced me to the minister and his advisors. One of them,
"Gerber," plopped down beside me and after some initial chitchat, outlined
the changes he wanted to one of the speeches. We discussed the edits and I
promised to send a new copy as soon as I got back to the office. He stood to
leave and said, "I almost forgot. We need you to prepare another speech for
tomorrow evening. The minister needs to speak for about ten minutes."
With that, he handed me six pages typed in Hebrew. "That's the content.
Can you turn it into a speech by this evening?" I swallowed and nodded.

I returned to the office, quickly made changes to the first speech and sent
it to Gerber. I then explained to one of our diplomats that I needed six pages
of notes translated ASAP, so I could prepare a speech. He made a phone call
and instructed me to return to the hotel where a member of the minister's
delegation would meet me to translate and help write the speech.

Over the next few days, I shuttled between the hotel, the United Nations,
and the office. The minister spent much of his time at the United Nations,

engaging in diplomatic speed dating. With so many ministers and heads of state in New York, the goal of every diplomat was to meet with as many others as possible to forge new relationships and strengthen old ones.

One afternoon, I was walking out of the hotel with Ron when we bumped into Canadian Foreign minister John Baird. The Canadian delegation was one of Israel's best friends at the United Nations and Minister Baird was an outspoken proponent of Israel, coming to its defense on numerous occasions. Ron walked over to him and exclaimed, "John, it's good to see you. You need to meet my speechwriter, Aviva. She's Canadian."

Grateful he didn't attempt to say the minister's last name, I stepped forward.

Baird shook my hand and said, "It's nice to meet you. You should meet my speechwriter. He's Israeli," and he pointed to a young man standing nearby.

I walked over to shake his hand and asked if he was in fact Israeli.

He laughed and explained he was both Israeli and Canadian but was actually Baird's director of policy rather than a speechwriter. I was delighted by the chance encounter and the unlikely coincidence of a Canadian working for the Israelis and an Israeli working for the Canadians.

———————

Earlier in the month, Ron had told me he wanted to write an op-ed about the new Iranian president. He wanted to argue Rouhani was far from a moderate leader and Iran's real decision-maker, Supreme Leader Ayatollah Ali Khamenei, remained committed to acquiring nuclear weapons that threatened Israel. He reasoned that the arrival of Rouhani in New York presented the perfect opportunity to place the article in a major American newspaper. I set to work drafting the op-ed. I knew the article would be more appealing to editors if we released it the day before Rouhani spoke to the General Assembly; even more so if we used the article as a preemptive opportunity for

Israel to explain why its ambassador would step out of the Assembly when Rouhani rose to speak. The problem was we still did not have a decision from Jerusalem as to whether Ron should stay in the room. As the day drew closer, I realized the decision would probably be made only hours before Rouhani was scheduled to speak. From the discussion in the office, I guessed that Ron would be instructed to stay out of the room, so I set to work redrafting the op-ed to explain why Ron had walked out.

That evening, I was sitting in my office when I got a phone call from Gerber asking me to come over to the hotel to finish off a speech for the following morning. I collected a laptop and headed over, arriving just after nine o'clock. I made my way upstairs past the imposing security guards. Ron was standing in the hallway. I handed him the latest draft of the op-ed and he read it over. When he was done he handed it back and explained that he wanted to change the focus somewhat. He gave me a list of changes and instructed me to send him a new draft when I was finished at the hotel. It was going to be a long night.

One of the minister's advisors found me waiting in the hall and told me the minister was concluding a meeting. He directed me to a nearby room and said he'd be back as soon as they were ready. I flipped on the television and waited. An hour later, the advisor reappeared and escorted me into the minister's suite where he was sitting with a handful of other advisors. I distributed hard copies of the speeches to everyone in the room.

The minister began reading aloud, but barely made it through a sentence before one of the advisor's interjected and asked if this was how he wanted to start the speech. They debated for a while and then continued. The minister read another sentence and was interrupted by someone else asking if the phrasing was correct. This sparked a discussion of word choices. Twenty minutes had passed, and we were still in the first paragraph of the first speech. As they crawled through, I listened in horrified amazement as the small group of Israelis debated word choices, expressions, and turns of phrase, using both Hebrew and broken English. As the only native English speaker in the room, I was tempted to interject, but the last thing anyone needed was one more voice in the room.

Two hours later, the minister lost patience with the endless debates and decided he would dictate what he wanted. He slowly recited what he wanted to say. When one of the advisor's interrupted, he shot her a dirty look and continued. He was not fully at ease speaking in English, so he thought carefully about each word he would use. The sentences were a bit muddled, so I corrected the grammar as I typed out his instructions. When he was done, he stood, stretched, and thanked me. I took that as my cue to leave and two advisors walked me out of the suite.

"What about the other two speeches?" I asked.

"We will have to go through them tomorrow." Gerber answered, "Right now, we need to go through this speech one more time and polish it up a bit."

It was already well past midnight, but I walked with Gerber down the hall, sat at the computer, and began reading back what the minister had dictated. Gerber made some suggestions and changes. Bleary-eyed, I worked on a section denouncing the death of two IDF soldiers by terrorists the previous weekend. I had typed, "We denounce this trajic act of terror." The cursor blinked beside "trajic" and I stared at the word, knowing the spelling was wrong. Yet, try as I might, I could not make my brain conjure the correct spelling.

Forty-five minutes later we went to the hotel business center to print copies of the speech. I passed the copies to Gerber and said goodnight. I stepped out of the hotel into the cool fall evening and flagged a taxi to take me home. Exhausted, I dropped my bag at the door, sat down at my desk, and pulled up Ron's op-ed on Iran. With a resigned sigh, I set to work making the changes he requested. At two o'clock in the morning, I sent the revised op-ed to Ron and fell into bed.

The next morning, Ron received instructions that no Israeli should be in the General Assembly while Rouhani delivered his speech. The Israeli delegation planned to camp out in a side room to watch the speech projected live on a large screen. We gathered at the appointed time and listened to Rouhani declare "peace is within reach" if only the international community would recognize Iran's right to enrich uranium. He continued, "Sanctions, beyond any and all rhetoric, cause belligerence, war-mongering and human suffering."

These supposed overtures signaling cooperation ended abruptly when Rouhani turned his attention to the topics of Palestinians and Syria. While he never mentioned Israel by name, the intention of his comments was clear. "Apartheid as a concept can hardly describe the crimes and the institutional-ized aggression against the innocent Palestinian people," he decried.

I spent most of the next day camped out in a room at the United Nations working on the minister's last two speeches. Between meetings, the minister would come to the room to make phone calls and have a snack. When he arrived, my colleagues were herded out of the room, but I remained in place, huddling with his advisors to work through the speeches. In between, I sat with Ron and worked on his Iran op-ed. By this point, I had written around twenty drafts, and he still was not satisfied. He kept shifting the angle of the piece, and with each new draft his frustration grew. The long days were tak-ing a toll on his patience.

I was similarly frustrated. We had lost the chance to pitch the op-ed before Rouhani spoke and with the end of the day approaching, we were going to miss the chance to pitch the op-ed explaining why Ron had chosen not to hear the new Iranian president's inaugural address. The long hours and heavy demands were wearing on me. Irritable, I snapped at colleagues— particularly anyone who dared look over my shoulder at the computer to make suggestions about the piece. I was determined to finish and pitch the op-ed before leaving for the day. Seeing that I was on the verge of a meltdown, Keinan called Simonne and asked her to come help me out. She arrived and, seeing my sorry state, instructed me to pack up and go home. I wouldn't budge from the computer. She gently pulled the laptop away from me and reassured me she would be fine. Defeated, I stood and made Simonne promise to keep me posted on the changes and let me know if she got the go-ahead to pitch. Wearily, I walked out of the United Nations and made my way to the train. I sat down on the hard plastic seat and closed my eyes, trying to ignore the screech each time the train slowed down. When I finally got home, I fell into bed and slept for fourteen hours. I woke up feeling like myself again. Hopping out of bed, I reached for my phone and flipped through emails. Ron never gave Simonne permission to pitch the op-ed, and, unwilling to revisit the emotional rollercoaster, I never asked why. A few weeks later, we were contacted by a media outlet asking us for an opinion article on the Iranian president. I revived the article, updated it, and it was published on their website.

The next great challenge of the General Assembly was the arrival of Prime Minister Netanyahu. Ella, Dafna, and Keinan worked for weeks putting together a plan of military precision for the Mission staff. The prime minister was scheduled to address the General Assembly on the first of October, and hundreds of guests were invited to listen to him speak. Everyone in the Mission was given a job, and I was assigned to VIP escort duty. My instructions were to wait at the gates of the UN complex on First Avenue and escort high-profile friends of the prime minister into the Assembly. I escorted Alan Dershowitz and his wife inside the building and went back outside in time to see the prime minister's motorcade arrive. I watched the impressive entourage of military and diplomatic personnel parade into the building surrounding Prime Minister Netanyahu and his wife, Sara.

They made their way to a private room while my colleagues and I finished escorting guests inside. When I had seated the last guest, I went to the staff gathering point. Ella found me and said, "We're going to need a copy of his speech. So, grab a laptop and transcribe Bibi's words as he speaks."

"You have got to be kidding me." I replied, "I'm not a stenographer. There is no way I can type the speech as he delivers it. I'll never keep up."

"Well you have to, get one of the interns to do it as well and you can compare notes afterwards."

"Ella. Be serious. Can't you just ask the prime minister's staff for a copy of the speech after it's delivered?"

"They won't give it to us," she said.

"How is that possible?" I asked incredulously.

"I'm telling you they won't," and with that, she turned to deal with more pressing matters.

I went to find an intern and told him we were going to be typing out the speech. "Why can't we just get a copy from Netanyahu's staff?" he asked.

"Because we work for lunatics," I answered.

With a grim nod of understanding, he accepted the laptop and we made our way to a long table in the Assembly. Prime Minister Netanyahu approached the podium and began his remarks. We tried our best but typed barely a third of his speech. When the prime minister concluded, he was ushered to a receiving line to shake hands with diplomats and select guests. I stood near the front of the line watching. Ron was at the prime minister's side introducing him to his fellow ambassadors and dignitaries. He caught my eye and waved me over. He introduced me to the prime minister and we took a photograph together.

I left the line to find Ella and tell her she needed to come up with a new plan to get a copy of the prime minister's speech. Come to think of it, I probably should have told Netanyahu my dilemma as we posed for a photograph and asked him for the copy in his pocket. There was no need.

Within the hour, the prime minister's office released the speech online. Typical.

That evening, Dafna called to tell me the prime minister would be giving a briefing in the morning and Ron asked me to attend. I wrote down the details and the following morning arrived at the heavily guarded hotel and passed through security. One of my colleagues met me in the lobby and we went upstairs to a small room with a large table. Platters of muffins and fruit sat on the table alongside silver urns of coffee and tea. I looked at the place cards on the table and realized the briefing was for major media heads. Milling about the room were the presidents, chairpersons, editors, and anchors of the country's largest news outlets. Ron walked around the room chatting with some of the news personalities. A few minutes later, Prime Minister Netanyahu walked into the room escorted by half a dozen members of his entourage. He walked around the room, greeting and chatting with each of the invited guests and then took his place at the center of the table.

For thirty minutes, the prime minister spoke about the new Iranian president and the regime's efforts to advance its nuclear weapons program. When he opened the floor to questions, the assembled guests asked about his recent meeting with President Obama and how close Iran was to obtaining a bomb, and questioned the state of the Iranian economy. The prime minister was then asked if Israel was seriously considering military options against Iran. The questioner argued that any attack would create support for Iran throughout the Middle East. Netanyahu disagreed and told the following story:

Not long ago, I was invited to Uganda by President Yoweri Kaguta Museveni. He wanted me to attend a ceremony at the Entebbe airport terminal where Operation Entebbe took place. In 1976, the terminal was the site of a daring hostage-rescue mission carried out by commandos of the Israel Defense Forces. During the operation, the unit commander,

Lt. Col. Yonatan Netanyahu, my older brother, was killed. Now, almost forty years later, the airport terminal was being torn down, but a plaque would remain in the place where Yonatan died. After the ceremony, while speaking to Uganda's president, I said I was touched by the gesture, but couldn't understand why Uganda was willing to honor an operation that resulted in the death of 50-60 Ugandan soldiers. The president told me that he and his supporters had been fighting the regime for decades. When they heard that Israeli commandos flew over 2,500 miles and executed a successful rescue operation, they knew that the regime was not invincible. They knew they could change the course of the country.

The prime minister believed seventy to eighty percent of Iranians despised the regime. He said, "I think they are ready for change." And with that, he thanked the assembled guests and rose to leave.

After high-level week came the myriad meetings of the General Assembly and the UN committees. My interns and I worked every evening and most weekends to keep up with the writing demands. The speeches written during the summer seemed to cover most of what Ron and our local diplomats needed, but the horde of Israelis who arrived for the fall session needed an endless series of statements. Every day, they would pop their heads into my office telling me they "just needed" some remarks written, or they "just needed" me to review remarks written in Jerusalem.

Even though the UN schedule had been out for weeks, they waited until the last minute to let me know Jerusalem had not provided remarks and I would have to write them. Others would hand me remarks written in Jerusalem for review and I would discover they were riddled with incomprehensible sentences and grammatical errors. It was tiring work, and as the days wore on, my patience grew increasingly thin. Managing the speeches for one or two diplomats would have been fine but writing for Ron—who maintained his usual three to five speeches a week along with an endless array of letters—along with half a dozen demanding diplomats, who had no regard for one another's needs, had me exhausted.

Diplomats would saunter into my office, ignoring that I was deep in concentration on another assignment, take a seat beside me, and start outlining what he or she needed. They wanted to discuss their ideas for a new speech or the edits I had made to a speech written in Jerusalem. They could easily spend an hour discussing five-minute remarks, and I simply did not have the time, energy, or inclination. More than once, I barked that those were my edits and they could feel free to accept or reject them. Bewildered, they would leave my office and look for an intern to see if he or she would sit for an hour and debate the merits of the wording in a sentence.

By December, I was utterly worn out from the haphazard culture and heavy workload. After a particularly infuriating day dealing with last minute replies, I sat grumpily at my desk. Ron called me into his office and handed me a book. It was a compilation of speeches written by me and Avishai over the spring and summer. Avishai had bound the speeches into a book and given it as a gift to both of us when he left at the end of the summer. I had given my copy to Ron to inscribe weeks earlier and forgotten about it. He handed me the book and thanked me for all my hard work. Inside the cover he had written:

Dear Aviva

I will be the first to admit that it is not easy mastering the art of "Prosorism!" With time, devotion and a "little bit of tough love!" you are beginning to learn the three 's's—sense, sensitivity, and sensibility, coupled with humor.

Thank you for all your hard work. I hope we both will fill many more
volumes together which will speak volumes!

Big hug
Ron

I read the inscription and smiled. That small gesture went a long way in easing my fatigue and frustration.

———————

At the end of December, I promoted an intern to interim speechwriter and took off for Israel. I was staffing my eleventh Birthright trip. My plan had been to retire after my tenth trip, but I wanted to go to Israel while I was the Mission speechwriter. Once the participants found out about my job, they peppered me with questions, and I was happy to oblige with answers. As we crisscrossed Israel on our bus, I told them stories and described how my work at the United Nations overlaid the political situation they were learning about.

One evening, I was sitting in a hotel lobby in Tel Aviv looking at my Twitter feed when I saw a tweet from the Mission saying Ron was about to deliver remarks to the General Assembly. The participants were gathering in a nearby room waiting for our evening program to begin. I asked the front desk if I could use their computer. They swiveled the monitor around and I opened a web browser and found the United Nations' live webcast. Seeing that Ron would speak next, I went into the adjoining room and asked the group if they would like to watch Israel's ambassador deliver remarks I had written to the General Assembly. They jumped up, followed me into the lobby, and gathered around the monitor.

Iran had introduced a resolution entitled "World Against Violent Extremism" or WAVE. The act urged nations to take "appropriate measures to strengthen universal peace and to achieve international cooperation in solving international problems of an economic, social, cultural, or humanitarian character." It also encouraged "respect for human rights and for fundamental freedoms for all, without distinction of any kind such as to race, color, sex, language, religion, political or other opinions, national or social origin, property, birth, or other status."

Together, we watched Ron read out the statement I had written days before I left for Israel:

Mr. President,

Reading through the document before us, it wasn't clear to me if I was reading a UN resolution or President Rouhani's New Year's resolution.

After all, Iran is the world's primary sponsor of terror responsible for the murder of thousands of innocent civilians from Bangkok to Burgas and Buenos Aires. It is also the principal supplier of weapons in the Middle East, igniting conflicts and inflaming sectarian divides.

As Ron delivered the remarks, I watched my group as they watched the speech. We were joined by some of the hotel staff and they nodded in appreciation at Ron's words. It was a much-needed reminder of why my work mattered.

———

On January 11, 2014, former Israeli Prime Minister Ariel Sharon passed away at the age of eighty-five, after spending eight years in a coma. The son

of Russian immigrants, Ariel Scheinerman was born in 1928 on Moshav
Kfar Malal, about fifteen miles northeast of Tel Aviv. After high school,
he joined the Haganah, the underground Zionist fighting brigade that
later became the Israel Defense Forces (IDF). In 1947, he worked for the
Haganah on the Sharon Plain north of Tel Aviv. From there, and in the
Zionist tradition of Hebraizing diaspora names, he took a new Israeli last
name—Sharon.

At the height of Israel's War of Independence, Sharon's unit fought in the
battle of Latrun against the Jordanian Army, and he distinguished himself
as an outstanding soldier. Over the years, he rose through the ranks of the
IDF and eventually became a legendary military leader. After retiring from
military service, he pursued a career in politics, helping found the right-wing
Likud Party. In time, Sharon transitioned from a cunning military leader to
an astute politician. He earned the nickname "The Bulldozer" for his outspoken nature and determination to get things done. Sharon held nearly
every top government post before finally becoming prime minister in 2001
during the Second Intifada. At the time, daily life in Israel was gripped by
fear as waves of suicide bombers exploded in cafes, on buses, and in markets.
Sharon sent tanks and troops into Palestinian towns to root out militant
leaders. He also ordered construction of the separation barrier through the
West Bank and confined then-Palestinian-leader Yasser Arafat to his compound in Ramallah, for encouraging attacks on Israel. Bold and brash, Ariel
Sharon inspired intense reactions from both Israelis and non-Israelis. Sharon
adamantly believed Jews should unapologetically defend their collective
needs without fear of censure. As he wrote in his autobiography, "The great
question of our day is whether we, the Jewish people of Israel, can find within
us the will to survive as a nation."*

---

* Ariel Sharon and David Chanoff, *Warrior: An Autobiography*.

Sharon stunned both Israelis and the international community when, in 2005, he formed the centrist political party Kadima to build support for his plan to turn Gaza and parts of the West Bank over to Palestinian control. In 2005, he implemented the controversial disengagement from Gaza. A few months later he suffered a stroke that left him incapacitated.

News of Sharon's death came shortly before Ron was scheduled to deliver a Security Council speech. While I knew I had to mention Sharon in the speech, it wasn't easy to know what to write, given that he had been a polarizing figure. Ultimately, this is what Ron delivered:

> *Israel is proud of its democracy and yearns for peace with its neighbors and security in its borders. The people of Israel are still mourning the loss of their legendary statesman and soldier, Ariel Sharon. He was a fearless leader who knew the heavy price of war and was willing to take bold steps for peace. The State of Israel is still willing to take courageous steps for peace and is committed to serious and meaningful negotiations with the Palestinians.*
>
> [REMARKS TO THE SECURITY COUNCIL,
> JANUARY 2014]

The New Year brought with it good news for our delegation. Israel was invited to join the WEOG regional group in Geneva. Since 2000, Israel had been a part of WEOG at the UN headquarters in New York. However, the group's counterpart in Geneva had refused entry to Israel. The reversal in policy allowed Israel to normalize relations with UN bodies in Geneva and even, should it wish to do so, run for a seat on the UN Human Rights Council.

In February, 170 countries unanimously nominated Ron to chair elections for the UN Human Rights Committee. Not to be confused with the Human Rights Council in Geneva, the Committee monitors the implementation of the International Covenant on Civil and Political Rights by member states. A few weeks later, Israel was admitted in New York to JUSCANZ (The acronym stands for Japan, United States, Canada, Australia, and New Zealand, which were the group's original members), a UN voting bloc of the non-European states from the "Western" regional group of democracies. Both WEOG and JUSCANZ are groups where much of the behind-the-scenes coordination takes place for UN meetings, leadership assignments, and votes. For most of its history, Israel has been excluded from the United Nations' formal negotiating bodies and from its informal negotiating blocs, undermining its ability to participate in deliberations in committees. Israel's admittance into JUSCANZ was facilitated with support from the United States and was an important step forward for Israel to advance its national interests alongside like-minded countries and to begin to normalize its place in the family of nations. Ever so slowly Israel was chipping away at the biases in the UN system and finding small footholds. We disseminated a press release to the media celebrating Israel's entry into JUSCANZ, and a short while later a reporter on Twitter sent me the following message: "What can you tell me about Israel's involvement in 3rd committee today?"

I replied: "It was a good day for the good guys."

Within seconds, the reporter wrote back to let me know that he was looking for more details than what we had distributed in the press releases.

Deciding to have a little Ron-style fun, I tweeted: "Are you squeezing me for info on JUSCANZ or just peeling back the layers looking for juicy details?"

The reporter replied, "Both?"

"Well you won't get a drop out of me."

Picking up on the puns, he tweeted: "If the squeeze yields no juice, does the peel reveal slices?

"That sounds like Pulp Fiction."

"Or sour grapes."

I replied, "Bravo. That last one was a peach."

"Yeah, and I'm getting treated like the fuzz—stonewalled."

"I don't blame you for trying to get to the core of the issue."

"Yeah, well it rots."

"It's the pits," I concluded.*

As I reviewed the Twitter conversation, I realized that I should have just answered his question rather than start a pun war. It was clear I had succumbed to Ron's brand of humor.

———————

Around this time, I welcomed a new speechwriting intern named Erin to our ranks. Of all my interns, Erin probably has the most exciting story from her internship experience. One morning in January, I received instructions to write a letter of complaint to the Security Council. Overnight mortars had been fired from the Gaza Strip into Southern Israel. I wrote the letter, ran it through approvals, and Ron signed off. Normally I would send my intern to deliver a letter to the United Nations, but Erin had only started that same week and did not yet have the necessary pass. Eager to help, she borrowed a badge from a colleague, and headed over to the Secretariat building to deliver the letters. I got caught up in other work and an hour later realized she had been gone far too long. From my office, I heard a colleague around the corner set down the telephone and then remark aloud, "I wonder why Security

———————

* https://twitter.com/IlanBenZion/status/433366601606246400.

wants to see me." My heart sank as I put the pieces together. Just then, an email came through from Erin:

> *I got busted at the Secretary General's office. Fingers crossed everything will be fine, but I am currently surrounded by security and awaiting an "investigator" but it may take a while. They are worried about whether I got the pass willingly.*

Taking a deep breath, I rose from my seat and walked down the hall. I knocked on the deputy ambassador's office door and nervously told him my intern had been detained at the United Nations. It was so absurd that we both burst out in laughter. He quickly collected himself, looked at me sternly, and uttered a few words about the severity of the situation. He spent the next hour on the phone reassuring UN officials and security personnel that Erin was our employee and did not pose any sort of international threat. Hours later Erin was released and returned to the office in surprisingly good humor. The colleague who lent her badge had her UN credentials suspended for a few weeks, and I felt terrible about the episode. Needless to say, nobody borrowed badges again.

CHAPTER 8

Tzarat rabim chatzi nechama / Sorrow shared is sorrow halved

What are the steps in a diplomatic dance?

Early in the New Year, I tallied up the number of speeches I had written for Ron since I had started. I had been on the job 330 days and written one hundred speeches. That didn't include the numerous remarks I'd written for visiting ministers and diplomats. The good news was I was completing speeches in fewer drafts and spending far less time staring into space trying to think up one-liners. The real proof of how much I had progressed came when Ron asked me to write an op-ed about the treatment of Christians in the Arab world.

For two millennia, Christian communities dotted the landscape of the Middle East, enriching the Arab world with literature, culture, and commerce. At the turn of the twentieth century, Christians made up 26 percent of the Middle East's population. That figure has fallen to less than 10 percent as extremist governments drive away the Christian communities that had lived in the Middle East since their faith was born. A report by *Open Doors*, a nondenominational Christian not-for-profit, documenting the ten most oppressive countries for Christians to live in, found that nine were Muslim-majority states noted for Islamic extremism (the tenth being North

Korea).* These tyrannical regimes uphold archaic blasphemy and defamation of religion laws under the guise of religious expression.

I wrote the op-ed over the course of a week and took it to Ron, armed with a notepad and pen and ready to scribble down a long list of revisions and suggestions. He sat back in his black leather desk chair and read the article slowly. It was taking too long. Impatiently, I waited for him to put down the pages and offer feedback, but he continued to read. The silence was unsettling. I shifted in my seat as he turned a page and kept reading. With every page, I grew increasingly nervous. Eventually, he put the paper down, stood from his chair, came around the desk, and said, "Aviva Klompas, I need to give you a hug. It's perfect. Pitch it."

Shocked, I stood as Ron gave me a hug and thanked me for my hard work. Baffled and speechless, I walked out of his office and asked Dafna if Ron was feeling well.

"Why?" she asked.

"He approved a first draft of an op-ed I wrote. And then he thanked me and hugged me."

She stopped typing, looked up at me, and said, "That is weird. Don't ask questions, darling. Get it out the door."

I returned to my office, typed a note of explanation to the *Wall Street Journal*, and sent over the article. They were interested in taking it, but one of the Editorial staff wrote back asking that we elaborate on some of the points and provide sources to substantiate the piece. Over the course of a couple of weeks, I worked with the *Journal* to strip out much of the stuff Ron loved—the puns, word plays, and cynical retorts—and replaced them with statistics and references. When the *Journal* was finally satisfied, I reviewed the finished product. If I had handed Ron the version the *Journal* would be printing, he would have dismissed it out of hand as "snooze, snooze." The

* https://www.opendoorsusa.org/christian-persecution/world-watch-list/

article ran in the *Journal* over Passover and Easter and became the most-read article on the *Journal*'s website over the holiday weekend.

In April of 2014, the Obama administration learned what so many of its predecessors had come to understand: Washington cannot force, cajole, bribe, or otherwise incentivize an Israeli-Palestinian agreement. The previous July, Secretary of State John Kerry had set the goal "to achieve a final-status agreement over the course of the next nine months." His statement launched a diplomatic shuttle that would see him meet with Palestinian Authority president Abbas on thirty-four occasions, and about twice as often with Prime Minister Netanyahu.

His first six months were spent trying to address the core issues—guaranteeing Israeli security, drawing borders for a future Palestine, and deciding the fate of the Palestinian refugees and East Jerusalem. Failing to gain real traction, Secretary Kerry changed gears and sought to create a "framework for negotiations" that would outline the parameters on all core issues. In other words, he wanted to negotiate a plan to discuss *how* to discuss the most polarizing issues. This too yielded few results. Secretary Kerry then pushed the parties to extend the talks, or at the very least, continue talking about how to continue talking. A Middle East Security Council session was scheduled to take place on April 29, 2014, which was also the negotiation deadline. I began writing the speech two weeks in advance, but it proved to be a futile effort as events changed dramatically on an almost daily basis.

On April 1—April Fool's Day—Palestinian president Abbas signed fifteen UN treaties and international conventions. It was a provocative move of mostly symbolic value intended to infuriate the Israelis and irritate the Americans. The US administration had made agreements with the Palestinians that included a condition precluding them from signing international treaties. This was bad faith bargaining on the part of the Palestinians.

Ironically, the Palestinian leadership was in violation of at least eleven of the fifteen accords that Abbas signed. The Vienna Convention on Diplomatic Relations, for example, lays out the rules for foreign diplomats operating in a host country. In January 2014, Czech police found explosives, assault rifles, and handguns at the Palestinian mission in Prague, a direct violation of the Diplomatic Relations treaty.

The Convention on the Elimination of All Forms of Discrimination against Women calls on parties to end discrimination against women in all forms. UN reports detail the violence and honor killings to which Palestinian women are subjected.

The Convention on the Rights of the Child establishes protections for persons under the age of eighteen. Yet Hamas regularly trains children for military combat and terror operations to fight the Jews and destroy Israel. In 2013 alone, the group trained thirty-seven thousand children in urban warfare.

What followed was a series of diplomatic escalations. In response to the Palestinians signing the treaties and conventions, the Israeli government refused to release a group of Palestinian prisoners, who were set to be freed as a precondition of peace talks. Before coming to the negotiating table, the Palestinian leadership had demanded Israel release 104 convicted terrorists from its jails. The list included perpetrators of heinous crimes, including one who had murdered an elderly Holocaust survivor, another who had stabbed two Israeli teenagers, and another who had hurled a firebomb at a bus, killing a mother and her children. Israelis balked at the notion of setting murderers free, but the government was under considerable pressure to advance peace talks. Prime Minister Netanyahu had agreed to release prisoners in four stages over the talks' nine-month timeline. He didn't want Abbas to welcome home 104 "martyrs" on day one and then promptly abandon negotiations.

The Palestinian Authority was furious at Israel for refusing to release the final group of prisoners and responded by forging a political partnership with the Hamas terrorist organization. The two groups announced they would form a united government within five weeks and hold a presidential election in seven months. It was a highly inflammatory step. Fatah was signaling that it would sooner forge a pact with its primary political rival than negotiate with Israel.

The factions have been at ideological odds since Hamas was founded in 1987. Hamas is an Islamist group, while Fatah is largely secular. In 2007 there was a brief but bloody civil war between the two that left Hamas ruling 1.5 million Palestinians in the Gaza Strip and the Fatah-dominated Palestinian Authority governing the estimated 2.5 million Palestinians in the West Bank. The battle left 161 Palestinians dead and another 700 wounded. Hamas shot dozens of their enemies in the legs and arms at point blank range to ensure permanent disabilities. Since then, Hamas and Fatah have maintained a state of conflict, with reports of one group or the other jailing or torturing political opponents. From time to time, the two factions tried to reconcile. The groups had pledged to reconcile in Cairo in 2011 and Doha in 2012. Neither came to fruition. The 2014 pact would also dissolve within a few months.

The day after the Hamas-Fatah unity announcement, the Israeli Cabinet voted to suspend peace talks altogether. Israel flatly refused to negotiate with a government that included a terrorist organization committed to its destruction. Prime Minister Netanyahu set about shifting attention from the failed peace talks and toward a far more urgent priority, the advancement of Iran's nuclear program. The Iranians were on the cusp of signing an agreement with world powers that would give the regime sanctions relief without requiring them to dismantle a single centrifuge. Netanyahu told the press, "Despite the international preoccupation with Israel and the Palestinians, Iran's quest for a nuclear weapons capability is advancing before our eyes." He continued, "If this materializes, it will have enormously negative consequences for peace in the Middle East and for the entire world."

Every day brought a new and intense flurry of Middle East diplomacy. Trying to write Ron's speech was like trying to play darts on a small ship being tossed around in an angry storm—it was impossible to hit the target. On the Sunday before the Security Council meeting, Ella and I camped out at a coffee shop on the Upper West Side to finalize the remarks. In addition to being an astute political strategist, Ella seemed to inhabit a portion of Ron's brain. She knew exactly what Jerusalem needed us to say and how Ron would want to convey the message.

"Here's what we need to do," Ella said, taking off her reading glasses and leaning toward me. "We start with the peace talks, but we need to show that the Palestinians are playing the same game they always play. They demand concessions from Israel to come to the table and when it comes time to actually sign a deal, they run away. Worse, they run to Hamas or do something they know will kill the deal."

"Like a dance." I said.

"Exactly."

I started typing, "It's a tango. A two-faced tango."

"OK," Ella replied uncertainly. "What does that mean?"

"It means," I continued, "that when Israel tries to tango with Abbas, we find ourselves abandoned on the dance floor as Abbas waltzes off with Hamas."

"Love it. Now we're getting somewhere," came Ella's reply.

We worked out the sequence for the speech, cutting and pasting together sections I had written over the past two weeks and noting where I'd need to insert punchy lines for Ron. When we were done, Ella read every line out loud, slowly and meticulously analyzing and considering every word. While she made notes, I worked on the all-important one-liners. We worked late into the night refining sections until at last Ella was satisfied. We emailed the speech to Ron and parted ways to go home.

On April 28, the day before Ron was scheduled to deliver remarks to the Security Council, he called Israel's ambassador in Washington to get his input. Ella and I sat at Dafna's desk outside his office and listened to the conversation. I had written more caustic barbs than usual for Ron and I should have known it was a mistake to offer so many options. He was unwilling to part with any of them and the speech read like a bloated standup routine.

Fortunately, his Washington counterpart agreed. He offered a few suggestions for the content and then advised we drop most of the jokes. He suggested we keep just two. One on the international community rushing to embrace the Fatah-Hamas unity deal, "Some have even rushed to bless the Hamas and Fatah union faster than a Las Vegas marriage clerk." And a second, "Anyone who wonders why Israel won't negotiate with Hamas may as well be wondering why nobody shows up to dinner parties thrown by Hannibal Lecter."

After they hung up the phone, Ella and I trooped into Ron's office. We trimmed a few lines from the speech, but Ron was reluctant to cut many of the jokes. With a sigh, and a mental note to never again offer more than two or three jokes, I went to make edits to the speech. The following day, Ron delivered the speech to a crowded Security Council chamber.

Madam President,

When I think about the negotiations between Israel and the Palestinians, there is a predictable pattern on the part of the Palestinians—demand, delay and desert. Before taking a single step towards the negotiating table,

the Palestinian leadership demands that Israel submit to substantial con-
cessions. Once Israel agrees, they drag their feet and evoke every delay tactic
in the book. And then, as the deadline approaches and courageous leader-
ship decisions are required, Abbas deserts the talks.

He did so in 2008. After the Israeli prime minister offered an unprece-
dented and far-reaching peace deal, the Palestinians simply walked
away. He did it again in 2009. Prime Minister Netanyahu courageously
extended an olive branch to the Palestinians in his historic Bar-Ilan speech
and agreed to a ten-month settlement freeze. The Palestinians stalled and
did not reciprocate.

In February 2012—surprise, surprise—just as we were on the verge of a
breakthrough, Abbas abandoned the talks and flew to Doha to sign a unity
deal with Hamas, an internationally recognized terrorist organization.
And then, a few months later, the Palestinian leadership went to the U.N.
seeking to bypass direct negotiations.

[SITUATION IN THE MIDDLE EAST debate,
APRIL 2014]

Celebrating Israel's Independence Day at the United Nations alongside Ambassador Ron Prosor. (Courtesy of Shahar Azran)

During my first General Assembly, I spent most days camped out
in a room at the United Nations working on speeches.

Raphael, Nathan, and I dressed up as Winston Churchill,
whom Ron frequently quoted in his speeches.

Finalizing remarks with Ella for a late-night emergency
Security Council session during Operation Protective Edge.

Standing in the newly renovated Trusteeship Council Chamber. (Credit: © Rudi B Photography)

Ron invited me to meet President Shimon Peres when he visited New York.

We frequently gave press conferences following a major speech.

Jotting down notes while I sit in the General Assembly hall at the United Nations.

Brainstorming turned to joking as we discussed ideas for an upcoming speech.

At a dinner honoring President Shimon Peres, Ron gifted him with a backpack
and joked he could now do what every other Israeli does
when he finishes his national service—backpack through South America.

As soon as it was evident that Eyal, Gilad, and Naftali had been abducted,
Ron called a press conference demanding the United Nations condemn the abduction.

Nathan and I working on a speech with Ron and hoping he wouldn't denounce it as "shite."

Thousands of people gathered outside the United Nations
for a New York Stands With Israel rally.

Every year, UN Headquarters in New York welcomes over
one million visitors from around the world.

Following along as Ron delivers a speech I penned to the Security Council.
(Courtesy of the United Nations)

Listening to remarks from Israel's seat in the General Assembly hall.

A few hours before the J'accuse speech was to be delivered in the General Assembly, I was in Ron's office making edits. My father flew in to attend the speech and joined us for the review.

CHAPTER 9

Koev li halev / My heart hurts

What do you do when there's no other choice?

On June 12, 2014, three Israeli teenage boys, sixteen-year-olds Naftali Frankel and Gilad Sha'er, and nineteen-year-old Eyal Yifrach, went missing. The boys left school on a Thursday evening and made their way to the nearby bus stop. The teens waited at Geva'ot Intersection, west of the settlement of Alon Shvut in the Etzion Bloc south of Jerusalem. Naftali and Gilad lived in Nof Ayalon, about halfway between Tel Aviv and Jerusalem. The area is fairly remote and not serviced by direct bus or train lines, so the boys did what most students did each week to get home and hitchhiked. Around 9:30 p.m. Naftali texted his father to say he and Gilad were on their way home. His father, Avi Frankel, had gone to bed early and did not get the message for another hour. When he awoke at 10:30 p.m. he saw Naftali's text and sent back a short note before falling sleep.

At the bus stop, Naftali and Gilad waited for a ride along with a third boy, Eyal. Finally, a vehicle stopped, and all three boys climbed inside. At 10:25 p.m., Gilad dialed a police emergency number and whispered, "We've been kidnapped."

The call was transferred to a senior officer, who asked questions but received no reply. The call lasted for 2:09 minutes and was then cut off. The officer tried calling back repeatedly, before dismissing it as a prank. It took

some seven hours before security forces realized there had been a kidnapping
and launched a search operation.

At 3:30 in the morning, Avi Frankel was awakened by policemen knock-
ing on his door. Gilad's parents were looking for him. When he hadn't
returned home, they had called around and learned Naftali and Gilad had
left school together. They wanted to know if Gilad was inside. Avi and his
wife Rachel checked Naftali's room and found no sign of either boy. Worried,
Avi Frankel met Gilad's father, Ofir, and they drove to Gush Etzion early on
Friday morning to look for their boys. As time passed without word from
their sons, they knew something was terribly wrong.

It didn't take long for news to spread throughout the country and in international news outlets that three boys had gone missing and that the circumstances were considered suspicious. For eighteen days, Israelis and Jewish
people around the world prayed Eyal, Gilad, and Naftali would return home
safely. Vigils were held throughout Israel. Tens of thousands gathered at the
Western Wall in Jerusalem to pray and thousands more rallied in Tel Aviv's
Rabin Square. Millions of people around the world took to Twitter and
spurred a viral campaign to #BringBackOurBoys.

On June 30, 2014, the bodies of the three boys were found shot and bur-
ied in a shallow grave near Hebron. As news spread that the search had
ended in tragedy, the entire nation mourned the loss. Israeli television channels halted World Cup broadcasts and filled the airwaves with somber reflec-
tions, while radio stations played melancholy songs. Throughout the country,
heartbroken Israelis met on the streets to light candles, cry, and pray.
President Shimon Peres released a statement:

*All of Israel bows its head today. For 18 days, we hoped and prayed with
one voice that we would find the boys safe and well. With this bitter news,
all of Israel mourns their deaths. Along with our deep sense of loss we
remain committed to bringing the terrorists to justice. Our resolve in the*

fight against terror will only strengthen and we will ensure that murderous terrorism of this sort will not dare to rear its head again. At this difficult time, my thoughts and prayers are with the family. They educated their children with dedication and embedded within them a love of their country.

As days passed, the Israeli public's grief turned to outrage. Security forces had released the names and photos of the prime suspects, Amer Abu Aysha and Marwan Kawasme. The two were known to police, having previously served prison terms for their role with Hamas activities. Both men had been missing from their homes since the kidnapping took place. At first Hamas leaders denied any involvement in the kidnapping. Three months later, however, Hamas leader Khaled Mashal admitted his organization was behind the kidnapping and murders. On September 23, 2014, Israeli security forces located and killed Amer Abu Aysha and Marwan Kawasme in a house in Hebron. A third individual, Hussam Qawasmeh, was caught and confessed to planning the kidnapping and murders of the three teenagers. He was later convicted in an Israeli military court of three counts of premeditated manslaughter.

During the eighteen-day search for Eyal, Gilad, and Naftali, nearly two thousand Palestinian homes and institutions were searched and about four hundred people were detained, most of whom were affiliated with Hamas. Tensions escalated, and Palestinian street protests erupted in opposition to Israel's actions and as a show of solidarity with Hamas.

On July 2, a small, slightly-built, seventeen-year-old Palestinian boy named Mohammad Abu Khedair waited on the corner for some friends to go together to dawn prayers at the local mosque, a few blocks away. While

Mohammad waited, a car pulled up alongside him. A struggle ensued, and the boy was wrestled into the car before it sped off.

Mohammad's mother, Suha, knew something was wrong when Mohammad's cousin knocked on the door and asked his whereabouts. Unable to reach her son on his cell phone, Suha called the police. In the car, a terrified Mohammad continued to struggle with his abductors, desperate to get away.

One of the kidnappers, a Jewish man named Yosef Haim Ben-David, drove to the Jerusalem forest and pulled his captive from the car. Mohammad was beaten unconscious with a crowbar while his attacker screamed revenge for the murders of Eyal, Gilad, and Naftali. They doused Mohammad's beaten body with gasoline and set him on fire.

At 10 a.m., Mohammad's father, Hussein Abu Khdeir, heard a report on an Israeli radio station that a burned body had been discovered in a forest and had a terrible premonition that it was his son.

Police arrested Yosef Haim Ben-David and two other perpetrators, whose names were withheld under a court order because they were sixteen, the same age as Mohammad. News of Mohammad's death triggered riots in East Jerusalem. At the same time, Hamas in Gaza responded by firing rockets at Israel. As the days passed, tensions and violence continued to escalate. Hamas and Palestinian Islamic Jihad continued to fire hundreds of rockets into Israel. They reached as far as Jerusalem, Tel Aviv, and Haifa. For days, air raid sirens sounded almost continuously throughout the country.

_____

On July 8, 2014, Israel launched "Operation Protective Edge" with the stated goal of restoring quiet to Israel by halting Hamas rocket fire into Israel. The objective expanded nine days later when thirteen heavily armed Hamas terrorists from Gaza emerged from a tunnel into an open field outside an Israeli kibbutz. Fortunately, the IDF foiled the attack.

According to the Shin Bet, Israel's Security Agency, Hamas had begun building tunnels as early as 2000. One of these tunnels was used in 2006 by Hamas fighters to sneak into Israel, ambush an army patrol, and kidnap Gilad Shalit, a nineteen-year-old soldier. Shalit was held captive in Gaza for five-and-a-half years, until Israel agreed to free one thousand and twenty-seven Palestinian prisoners. For Hamas, this was proof the tunnels worked, and they set about building an intricate underground subterranean network.

Reports later showed the IDF had known about thirty-two tunnels but hadn't known that one third of them stretched inside Israel. They also hadn't comprehended the vast sophistication of the network that was stockpiled with weapons, Israeli uniforms, handcuffs, and tranquilizers, the gear needed to carry out attacks and kidnappings. Hamas would use its tunnel system to infiltrate Israel four more times before a cease-fire held.

Israel launched a ground offensive on July 17 to destroy the tunnels and impede Hamas's infrastructure and military capability. Operation Protective Edge lasted fifty days.

CHAPTER 10

Sof ha'olam smola /
At the end of the world, turn left

What do you do when no one will help you?

A s soon as it was evident that Eyal, Gilad, and Naftali had been abducted, our delegation called on the United Nations to denounce the kidnapping. Ron kept calling the Secretary-General's office until Ban Ki-moon agreed to condemn the abduction. The rest of the UN system was largely silent or dismissive. In a press conference, a UN spokesperson said the United Nations had no "concrete evidence" that three Israeli teenagers were "actually" kidnapped by Hamas terrorists. The statement was particularly galling, given the Secretary-General had already spoken out against the kidnapping and called for the boys' immediate release.

Even Palestinian president Abbas denounced the kidnapping. In an unusually courageous act, he addressed the issue in a speech to the Organisation of Islamic Cooperation in Saudi Arabia. His remarks were carried live on Palestinian television and other Arabic channels. President Abbas said, "Those who kidnapped the three teenagers want to destroy us." He continued, "They are human beings and we are looking for them and we will hold their kidnappers accountable, whoever they are."

By June 16, four days after Naftali, Gilad, and Eyal went missing, Ron was fed up with the United Nations' molasses-like response. Late in the day, he called some of his staff together and instructed us to hold a press conference the following day. Ella and I headed straight to my desk to write a media statement. In the morning, Ron read through the notes. Standing and pacing in his office, he grabbed a pen from his desk and scrawled new lines for me to type. We arrived at the United Nations and made our way to the media area in front of the Security Council chamber. Our media team had arranged to have an enlarged photo of the three teenagers on an easel behind the podium. With dozens of cameras rolling, Ron purposefully stepped to the microphone, glared into the cameras, and began:

It has been five days since our boys went missing. I ask the international community—where are you? Where are you?

The kidnapping took place just 10 days after Fatah and Hamas formed a unity government. All those in the international community who rushed to bless this marriage, should look into the eyes of the heartbroken parents and have the courage to take responsibility by condemning the kidnapping.

The international community bought into a bad deal and Israel is paying for it. We have gotten a taste of the bitter tragedy that comes with Hamas in a Palestinian government. Terrorism is what they know, it is what they preach, and it is what they teach.

[EXCERPT OF AMBASSADOR PROSOR'S MEDIA STAKEOUT ON JUNE 17, 2014]

Fired up, Ron continued his offensive. He directed me to write a strongly worded letter to the Security Council making clear that Israel was holding the Palestinian Authority responsible for the well-being of the kidnapped teens. "Remind the Council," he firmly instructed, "that the kidnapping took place just ten days after Fatah and Hamas formed a unity government."

The letter read:

Excellency,

Since 12 June 2014, the citizens of Israel have held their breath and waited to hear news of the Israeli teenagers kidnapped by Hamas terrorists. The three boys, 16-year-old Gilad Sha'er, 16-year-old Naftali Frenkel, and 19-year-old Eyal Yifrah, were taken captive while making their way home from school.

The Government of Israel holds the Palestinian Authority responsible for the wellbeing of the kidnapped teens. The kidnapping took place just 10 days after Fatah and Hamas formed a unity government. Israel has gotten a taste of the bitter tragedy that comes with Hamas in a Palestinian government. Terrorism is what they know, it is what they preach, and it is what they teach . . .

I call on the Security Council to immediately and unequivocally condemn the kidnapping. It must also call on President Abbas to disarm Hamas's military wing; halt the smuggling and manufacturing of weapons; and, stop the rockets fired from Gaza into Israel."

[LETTER TO THE SECURITY COUNCIL
ON JUNE 17, 2014]

Ron arranged to meet with the head of UNICEF and pointed out that for an organization purporting to represent the well-being of children, UNICEF had failed to denounce the kidnapping of three Israeli children. Officials interrupted and insisted that they had in fact issued a public statement. It took some time to figure out, but we eventually discovered the reference on UNICEF's social media sites. It took a while since their "statement" failed to use the words "kidnapping" or "condemnation."

Their Facebook post read: "Recent violent events affecting Palestinian and Israeli children underline the urgent need for stronger protection for children in the region." UNICEF also posted a tweet that read: "Children must never be targets or instruments of violence and conflict."*

That, apparently, was sufficient in UNICEF's eyes to condemn a kidnapping.

The following week, Ron asked us to arrange another press conference. Late in the day, he called me to his office, along with two members of the staff who were fluent in Arabic. He wanted to use a few lines of Arabic in his statement and asked them to suggest common expressions. They offered some ideas and Ron finally settled on using "*Darabni wu-Baka, Sabaqni wa-ishtaka*" which is Arabic for "He hit me and cried, he challenged me and complained."

I worked on the statement and sent a draft to Ron around midnight. When it came time for the press conference the following morning, I met Ron and Ella in the semicircular driveway in front of the UN Secretariat building. We made our way into the tall glass building and down to the lower level where we found a quiet place to review the statement. Ron, Ella, and I sat lined up on a bench. After reading through the notes, he turned to me and said, "You know what? I think I'm going to wing part of it."

"What's your plan?" Ella asked.

"The Arabs only understand strength, they only listen when it's about their honor," he replied. With that, Ron stood up and buttoned his suit jacket. We followed him, wondering what he would say. As we stepped off the escalator, Ron strode confidently toward the media gathered outside the Security Council. Reporters shouted questions, but he ignored them.

---

* https://twitter.com/UNICEFmena/status/478602252308201472

Standing before the cameras he calmly unfolded a paper and read the following.

While listening to the remarks made earlier by some of my colleagues, I'm reminded of an Arabic expression: Darabni wu-Baka, Sabaqni wa-ishtaka which means "He hit me and cried, he challenged me and complained."

He read a few more lines before pushing his notes aside and continuing:

Some nations give the world innovation, but the Arab nations give the world oppression and aggression. Remind me of a single innovation of the Arab nation in medicine or technology. The only innovation they have come up with lately is a single predictable pattern—coming together to demonize Israel, harass U.N. officials, and waste this body's time and resources.

Earlier today, you got another lecture from the representatives of Jeffersonian democracies. The lecture was brought to you by the U.N.'s own odd couple—Iran and Saudi Arabia. Back home, they are fighting a proxy war in Syria, but here at the U.N., love is in the air. [sings a few bars of "Love Is in the Air"] Unbelievable. They have one thing in common: both are cradles of terrorism and radicalism in the Middle East. One created Hezbollah and the other created Al-Qaeda.

[Excerpt of Ambassador Prosor's media
stakeout on June 17, 2014]

As I watched from the sidelines, my phone buzzed. Simonne texted me from the office, "Am I actually watching him sing, 'Love Is in the Air??' at a press conference?"

You better believe it.

Day after day, rockets were fired from Gaza, and Israel responded with air-strikes against Hamas targets. The Iron Dome missile defense system shot down many of the rockets, preventing devastating casualties on the Israeli side. The famed one-billion-dollar program is the short-range component of Israel's anti-missile defenses. When enemy rockets are launched, Iron Dome's radar tracks their trajectory, calculates their impact point, and launches a missile, which within seconds, locks onto the rocket and blasts it into harmless pieces in the sky. It's a marvel of engineering technology akin to trying to hit a speeding bullet with another speeding bullet in midair.

Each interception rocket reportedly costs around sixty thousand dollars, so Iron Dome only deployed when a rocket was projected to land in populated areas. The system was reported to be around 85 percent successful at preventing rockets from landing in populated areas. Even so, much of the country was paralyzed by non-stop rocket alerts. Depending on where Israelis lived, they had between fifteen and ninety seconds to reach a bomb shelter. With sirens sounding dozens of times a day throughout the country, the public was demanding its government act to restore quiet in the country. On Monday, July 7, Gaza terrorists fired approximately eighty rockets at Israel in a single day. The following day, Hamas fired some 150 rockets. Over the next ten days, Hamas launched around 1,500 more rockets, even as Israel's air force and navy retaliated against targets inside Gaza. I had an app on my phone called "Red Alert" which notified me every time a rocket or mortar was fired into Israel. It buzzed non-stop.

In the office, I received instructions to write a letter urging the Security Council to condemn the rocket fire. By this point, I had probably written

fifty of these letters, so I quickly prepared a draft using the standard language. I gave it to Ella who checked the tone was firm without being inflammatory. We brought the draft to Ron's office and I passed it to him. I sat
across from him and watched as he balled it up.

"This is all wrong," he started. "Write a letter that says enough is enough."

Unclear what he meant, I looked over at Ella. She nodded at Ron and
stood up.

We walked out of the room together and she stopped me at the door, put
a hand on my arm, and instructed. "Go do it quickly. Something is about to
happen."

From his office, Ron called, "Hurry up. That letter has to get to the
UN now."

A short while later I returned to Ron's office with a new draft. He pulled
out his green ink pen and signed.

"Have it delivered immediately," he instructed as he passed it back to me.

*As I write this letter, rockets are falling relentlessly on major Israeli cities
including Be'er Sheva, Ashkelon, Ashdod, and Beit Shemesh while sirens
are sounding in the areas around Tel Aviv and Jerusalem. Hamas is indiscriminately targeting millions of innocent men, women, and children deep
in the heart of Israel. With only seconds to run for cover, Israelis will spend
the night sleeping in bomb shelters. Day camps and businesses in Southern
and Central Israel have closed and the streets are deserted. In a single hour
earlier today, Hamas and other terrorists fired over 65 rockets towards
Israeli homes, schools, and hospitals—that is one rocket per minute. Over
the weekend, Israel offered Hamas a ceasefire and was met with hundreds
of rockets in exchange.*

*Israel will no longer tolerate this situation. Those who target Israelis with
terrorism will pay a very heavy price. Hamas has taken responsibility for*

the barrage of rockets. The Israeli government will now fulfill its responsibility by defending its citizens. We will put a stop to these terrorist attacks; it is our duty as a responsible government to do so.

[EXCERPT OF AMBASSADOR PROSOR'S LETTER
TO THE SECURITY COUNCIL ON JULY 7, 2014]

A few hours later, the Israeli Government launched Operation Protective Edge to stop Hamas's unrelenting rocket attacks against Israel's civilians. The following morning, the American national news programs called, inviting Ron to appear on their show. Ron, Anat, Ella, and I sat together and discussed the messages he should convey on the show. As we batted around ideas, our phones beeped and vibrated with Red Alert notifications. Suddenly I had an idea. "Ron, when you're on television rest your phone on your leg. If you see a rocket alert, hold your phone up to the camera and explain that as you speak, rockets are being fired into Israel."

On the way to the studio, Anat and I reviewed a page of media messages, peppering Ron with tough questions that he may be asked. When we arrived at CNN's offices overlooking Columbus Circle, we were led toward the studio. We walked down the corridors lined with large, glossy photos of CNN personalities. I continued asking Ron questions as he sat in the makeup chair and then had a sound tech clip a microphone to his suit. As we walked onto the set, I reminded him to keep his phone on his leg and hold it up for the camera if there was an alert. As it happened, there were no rocket alerts while Ron was live on-air. But he was not going to miss the opportunity to deliver the message. At one point during the interview, he held up his iPhone and explained about the app. From outside the studio where I was watching the broadcast, I held my breath. Ron kept holding his phone in the air in case there would be an alert, so it could be broadcast live. He held it up so long I worried it was starting to look like an advertisement for the iPhone. As he continued to wave the phone toward the camera, I was struck by a horrifying thought. What if he got a text from the prime minister's office as he was holding up his phone and waving it in the air? Or worse, a personal message from his wife or kids?

I paced nervously until Ron eventually gave up and put his phone back down. As the interview wrapped up and the program went to commercial, my phone vibrated notifying me of a rocket alert.

In the first ten days of the operation, 1,497 rockets were launched at Israel, of which 1,093 landed in Israel (another 301 were intercepted by the Iron Dome and a few landed inside Gaza). Friends in Israel described having to wake their children in the middle of the night and run to a shelter. Others were fearful of taking a bus or driving a car because if there was a siren, they would have to get out and lie flat on the road. It was surreal to imagine these things. The situation was far more difficult for my colleagues. Many had family members living in Beersheba, Ashkelon, Ashdod, and other southern communities where the rockets were falling continuously.

Sitting in the office one afternoon, I asked a colleague if he was in favor of the government launching a ground invasion to put an end to the rocket fire. I assumed he would be opposed because a ground invasion would most certainly mean Israeli casualties. In a tiny country like Israel, the grief of losing a soldier is felt across the country. He surprised me by adamantly arguing in favor of a ground operation, explaining, "Israel can't live with the constant threat of Hamas. We have seen this before. In early 2000, there were dozens of terrorist attacks. The whole country was on edge, but it wasn't until Passover of 2002 when a terrorist killed a crowd of people in a hotel that we finally retaliated."

He was referring to the March 2002 attack on the Park Hotel in Netanya. During the Passover dinner, a Hamas suicide bomber disguised as a woman walked into the dining hall and blew himself up, killing twenty-nine people and injuring 140. For almost a year and a half, Palestinian terrorism from the West Bank and Gaza Strip had become a daily scourge on Israeli life. Suicide bombers blew themselves up in cafes and on busses. Snipers fired at Israeli cars on the highway and planted improvised explosive devices (IEDs) along the road. From September 2000 through the end of February 2002, nearly three hundred Israelis were murdered by Palestinian terrorists. The Passover attack was the final straw. Hamas claimed responsibility and Palestinian officials lauded the attack in Arabic media. Then-Prime Minister Ariel Sharon green-lighted an operation, explaining to the Israeli public in a March 31 address:

> *Citizens of Israel, the State of Israel is in a war, a war against terror. This is a war that was forced on us. It is not a war we decided to embark upon. This is a war for our home . . . We must wage an uncompromising fight against this terror, uproot these weeds, and smash their infrastructure because there is no compromise with terror. It is impossible to compromise with someone who is prepared—like the suicide-bombers on the streets of Israel's cities and at the World Trade Center in the U.S.—to die in order to kill innocent civilians, children, women, and infants, to die in order to cause fear and terror.*

Operation Defensive Shield was a large-scale military operation against Palestinian terrorists in the West Bank. Israeli forces went into large Palestinian cities like Ramallah, Tulkarm, Qalqilya, Jenin, and Nablus, as well as many small towns and villages, and conducted house to house searches for terrorists and weapons. Thirty IDF soldiers were killed during the month-long mission and more than 120 were wounded in fierce urban fighting.

The result, as reported by the Israeli Intelligence and Terrorism Information Center, was a 46 percent drop in the number of suicide bombings. The IDF also reinforced its presence in the West Bank and significantly improved its ability to track and apprehend suspected terrorists.

My colleagues believed the government needed to conduct a similar operation in Gaza, sending soldiers door to door to arrest terrorists and uncover weapons caches. According to polls reported in Israeli media, most Israelis agreed and were pressing the government to take decisive action to end the rocket fire once and for all.

Israelis had been living with rockets from Gaza for almost a decade. In 2005, Prime Minister Sharon announced a Disengagement Plan in which Israel would unilaterally withdraw from the Gaza Strip. Sharon declared the withdrawal would increase the security of residents of Israel, relieve pressure on the IDF, and reduce friction between Israelis and Palestinians.

Israel turned Gaza over to the Palestinians, along with four communities in the northern West Bank. Thousands of Israeli families were uprooted from their homes and their businesses dismantled. By the time they were done, there was not a soldier, not a settler, not a single Israeli left in Gaza. They left behind greenhouses and other agricultural structures Palestinians could use to develop the Palestinian economy. To help Gaza succeed, Israel opened border crossings and encouraged commerce in the hopes the disengagement would serve as a model for two societies to live alongside one another in peace.

Within months of Israel's disengagement, civil war broke out between Hamas and Fatah. Hamas destroyed the greenhouses and businesses and, rather than build economic institutions, it built a terrorist regime. Within two years, Hamas had full control of Gaza and in almost every month since, has fired rockets toward Israel's towns and cities. Over time, it expanded its arsenal of rockets from a few hundred to thousands. The weapons they have today are more sophisticated and can reach farther into Israel than ever before.

Every few years, Hamas escalates its attacks by launching a massive offensive. Each time, the rockets and missiles are more sophisticated and are able to reach further into Israel. In 2008, over the course of three weeks, Hamas fired eight hundred rockets that could reach one million Israelis living in the area near Gaza. In 2012 Hamas fired 1,200 rockets in a single week that could reach 3.5 million Israelis in southern and central Israel. By the summer of 2014, Hamas had fired 3,800 rockets that threatened five million Israelis—or 70 percent of the population—living throughout the country. After each escalation, the international community brokered a cease-fire that Israel accepted, hoping it would finally bring peace. Yet, after three rounds of major assaults and more than twelve thousand rockets, it was abundantly clear Hamas was not interested in bringing quiet to Gaza. The terror group is openly and unapologetically committed to its 1988 charter which spouts conspiracy theories and anti-Semitic tropes to justify its calls for the destruction of Israel.*

———————————

As fighting continued in Gaza, we were inundated with media requests. Ron spent days going from studio to studio giving interviews. Local Jewish organizations also sprang into action. One had the idea of sending a letter to every UN ambassador explaining Israel's right to self-defense. Ron thought it was a great plan and somehow the job of writing the letter landed on my desk. As nice an idea as it was, I was struggling to keep up with the long list of writing requests members of the delegation needed. Protesters sporadically gathered and rallied in front of the Israeli mission. Each time, security wouldn't allow us to leave the building until the crowd dispersed. Frequently, we were trapped inside, unable to go out for food or have meals delivered to the building.

———————————

* http://avalon.law.yale.edu/20th_century/hamas.asp

Well-wishers take note: don't send letters to ambassadors, send pizza for the staff of the Israeli delegation.

On July 9 we learned Riyad Mansour, head of the Palestinian delegation, planned to hold a press conference at the United Nations. Unwilling to let him dominate the news cycle, Ron decided that he would do the same. He instructed me to prepare a statement reminding the public that Hamas had started the most recent escalation, and by refusing every cease-fire offer and indiscriminately firing rockets into Israel, the terror group was prolonging the conflict. Ron concluded his instructions saying, "I need to convey that no government and no nation in the world would tolerate attacks of this nature on their citizens."

An hour before he was scheduled to speak, I handed Ron his statement. He was deeply unhappy with the draft and barked new instructions. I scribbled furiously on a pad of paper struggling to keep up. Seeing me lag behind, he snapped, "We're going to your office to make the changes on your computer."

Ella in tow, we marched over to my office. For the next hour, he dictated and revised until there was a draft that met his approval. By the time we were done, we only had a few minutes to get over to the United Nations. I hit print and as the papers came rolling out of the printer, I grabbed my UN pass and some other things we would need because we had to go straight from the press conference to an interview at Bloomberg News. Ella grabbed the pages off the printer and I stapled them together. We hurried to meet Ron in the car and drove over to the United Nations. As we strode quickly through the corridors to the press room, I handed Ron his statement.

We arrived to find most of our delegation and a few dozen reporters seated in the room. Ron walked to the front of the room, took the notes I had handed him from his pocket, and placed them on the podium. I stood at the side of the room and watched. A few seconds into his remarks, he paused and stumbled over a sentence. I looked toward the podium and could see he was scanning the page in front of him in confusion. I looked down at my own version and a second later it dawned on me that there had probably been an old version of the statement on the printer and it had gotten mixed in with the new one.

My blood turned to ice. Ron would be furious—and rightly so. I snuck around the room to where Ella was sitting in one of the press seats. I knelt beside her and whispered, "We have a bit of a situation."

"What is it?" she asked distracted as she texted on her phone.

"Ron has the old version of the statement."

Ella's head snapped up. "What?" she said a little too loudly.

"Shhhh," I muttered, "He doesn't have the new draft."

"He's going to kill us," Ella said slowly, growing noticeably paler.

She stood up and we both ducked behind a pillar near the door. Huddled out of Ron's eyesight, I said, "Forget the Red Alert app. You know what we need? We need a Ron Alert. This is a dangerous situation."

The pressure and lack of sleep was affecting all of us, and Ron was no exception. He had been short-tempered all week. I peered around the pillar and listened to the statement. Ron seemed to remember many of the sections he had dictated by heart. When he finished delivering the statement, he took questions while Ella and I, still hiding out of his eyesight behind the pillar, debated who was at fault.

"You handed him the statement," she said.

"Yeah, but you took the wrong one off the printer."

"Why didn't you tear up the old version?"

"I didn't have a spare second to think—we went straight from Ron's office to my office to here."

We both grew silent as our spokesperson stepped to the microphone and announced the press conference was over.

Ron walked to the back of the room, pointed at us, and, in a fierce voice, said, "I'm going to deal with you two."

Blessedly, there was a reporter waiting to interview Ron and they stepped into a quiet nearby passageway to talk for a few minutes. Nearby, I shifted nervously, fearful of what was to come. When Ron was done with the reporter he joined us and before he could say a word, Ella jumped in and said, "Before we deal with the statement, let me give you all the updates." She began chattering at him in Hebrew as we made our way downstairs to the car. She managed to continue talking for long enough to shift Ron's focus away from the press conference. When she was done, she ended by saying, "Aviva, prep Ron for the interview at Bloomberg."

I launched into a description of where we were going and the questions likely to be asked. After a few minutes, Ron got a call on his cell and as he settled back in his seat to chat on the phone, Ella and I let out a sigh of relief. It looked like we had dodged a very angry bullet.

Bloomberg News is easily my favorite news studio. Aside from the fact the reporters aren't overtly hostile to Israel, they have a wonderful open-air vestibule where staff and guests can gather to snack. There is a drinks section with sodas and a coffee bar. Another area is stocked with cereals, oatmeal, breakfast bars, and fruit, another has fruit and nuts, and another has all sorts of healthy chip and pretzel snacks. When our interview was over, we strolled between the various stands munching away. I drifted over to the coffee stand to make a latte. When I returned, Ella said, "There's going to be an emergency Security Council session. We need to go back to the office and you need to get writing."

I grabbed a few fruit bars and we headed back to the car.

CHAPTER 11

Gam Elohim boche / God also cries

Does God also cry?

W hen we returned to the office, there was a flurry of activity. A "War Room" was being set up to serve as a central location for staff to gather and coordinate the flow of information between Israel and New York. I went to my office to draft a speech for the emergency session of the Security Council. Within a couple of hours, I had most of the speech prepared, but it needed something to make it memorable. As always, Ella insisted on drama. She sat with me in my office and we batted around ideas.

Dafna called to say Ron wanted Israel's ambassador in Washington to look at the speech when it was ready. I sent it off to him with a note that we were still working on a bold idea for the introduction. I rounded up some colleagues to join me in my office for a brainstorming session and we dug up a bottle of liquor. After a couple of warm-up shots, we tossed around ideas, searching for the perfect hook. Our phones vibrated and beeped intermittently alerting us of rockets falling in Israel.

My colleague Maayan suggested Ron begin by slowly counting out loud to fifteen to give Security Council members a sense of how little time Israelis living near Gaza had to reach a bomb shelter. Testing the idea, I started counting out loud. Fifteen seconds is an absurdly short amount of time to run for cover, but it's interminably slow when counted slowly out loud.

Half-jokingly, I offered, "A better idea would be for us to play a real siren."

Heads shot up. We looked at each another and realized that we may have found our idea.

Maayan grabbed her phone and opened the Red Alert app, explaining it has a feature in the settings to play the sound of a siren. We listened to it wail and knew we had our introduction.

I drafted the text to introduce the siren, then Ella and I went through the speech line by line perfecting every sentence. While we were working, the ambassador in Washington replied to my email suggesting we open the speech by playing a siren. Clearly, we were on the right track. We worked late into the night finishing the speech and getting the necessary approvals.

The following morning, we sat with Ron and had a final read-through of the speech. We explained how to make the siren sound from his phone app. Ron was worried it would take too long for him to get it to play or he'd encounter some technical issue. We decided I would sit behind him and hand him my phone with the siren sounding at the appropriate moment and he would place it next to his microphone. We were running late and arrived in the Security Council Chamber without having a chance to practice the phone siren to ensure we got the timing right. When it came time for Ron to speak, I sat nervously behind him and listened to him read the first few lines of the speech. As he concluded the first paragraph, I turned on the siren and passed him my phone.

Mr. President,

As I speak, there is a storm of rockets being fired by the Hamas terrorist organization in Gaza. Hamas is intentionally and indiscriminately threatening the lives of three and a half million innocent men, women, and children in Israel from north to south—from Beersheba to Tel Aviv to

Haifa. In the last three days, 442 rockets have been fired into Israel— that's one every ten minutes.

Fifteen seconds [play sound of siren]. That's how much time you have to run for your life. Imagine having only fifteen seconds to find a bomb shelter. Now imagine doing it with small children or elderly parents or an ailing friend.

A generation of Israeli children is growing up under the shadow of this threat. This abnormal way of life has become the "normal" way of life for many Israelis—and it is absolutely unacceptable. No nation, no people, and no government could tolerate this.

[EXCERPT OF AMBASSADOR PROSOR'S SPEECH
TO THE SECURITY COUNCIL ON JULY 10, 2014]

That fifteen second siren became my fifteen seconds of fame. The clip was played and replayed on international news stations. I got emails and phone calls from dozens of people saying they had seen me on television handing my phone to the ambassador. That afternoon, I went with Ron to do the news rounds. Every major outlet wanted to interview him. We rushed from Al Jazeera to CNN International to CNN America. I returned to the office late in the afternoon, famished. Trooping over to the kitchen, I opened the fridge and studied its sad contents. Aside from condiments, all I could find was a rather bruised avocado. My stomach growled, so shrugging, grabbed the avocado, cut it open and headed back to my desk to continue working, all the while thinking longingly of the Bloomberg snack stations.

———

In the coming days, my colleagues and I worked around the clock. It was not uncommon for me to be at work until the early hours of the morning, go home to sleep for two or three hours, shower, and return to work. I walked around with dark circles under my eyes and seemed to be perpetually fighting off a cold. A few friends took note of my sleepless nights and sent Starbucks gift cards. One in particular made me chuckle. It featured the American stars and stripes and read "Thank you for serving our country." My friend Susan added a note: "Right message, wrong flag."

By July 17, I was thoroughly worn down and battling a horrible cold. The morning was relatively quiet, so I left shortly after lunchtime to pick up chicken soup and go home to rest. As I arrived at my apartment, my phone started to buzz incessantly. I checked my messages and learned Israel had sent troops into Gaza. A ground invasion had begun. Without putting my bag down, I turned and headed back to midtown. When I got to the office, I walked straight into the War Room, dropped my bag, and announced to no one in particular, "I leave for an hour and you invade Gaza?" Nobody even looked up from their computers. Picking up my bag, I turned and went to my office to work on a new speech. Ella was certain the Security Council would call an emergency session. By early evening we got word there would be an emergency session in the morning.

We soon learned that IDF soldiers were encountering all manner of boobytraps inside Gaza. Entire houses were rigged with explosives and the army was discovering tunnels hidden in private homes and mosques. The IDF focused its activity on the town of Shejaiya, where the intelligence services identified four major tunnel networks that led to Israeli kibbutzim.

Several staff offered to help me gather content for the Security Council speech and we all set to work. I moved to a computer in the War Room and, with eight others looking on, worked on the speech. Predictably, this turned out to be a less than productive approach. It didn't help that my sinuses were clogged, and my head felt heavy and foggy. A colleague went out to pick up pizza for dinner, and I washed mine down with slugs of cold medication.

Someone had the idea that Ron should take a large compass along to the

Security Council and say something about the Council having lost its way and needing to find new direction. Keinan offered to hunt down a compass as I continued to draft remarks. At two o'clock in the morning, I decided it was time to go home and get some rest. Before I left, I sent an email to the office of Rabbi Lord Jonathan Sacks. I have been a fan of Rabbi Sacks for years and had met one of his staff members, Dan, a few weeks earlier. Dan offered that if we ever needed help, I should send a note. I wrote to let him know we would be giving a speech to the Security Council in the morning and wanted to include a passage from the Torah conveying that Israel didn't ask for this conflict. Rather, in the face of unrelenting attacks against its citizens, it was left with no choice.

When I arrived at work in the morning, I was delighted to find a response with the perfect quote from the Book of Psalms: "Too long have I lived among those who hate peace. I am for peace; but when I speak, they are for war."

I was inserting the passage into the ending of the speech when a couple of diplomats came into my office with a pile of notes they wanted incorporated into the speech. My head swam as I listened to their ideas and scribbled down their notes. When they were done, they looked at me expectantly. I shooed them out of my office and got to work. An hour later, the speech was ready. We sent it to the ambassador in Washington who sent back some helpful suggestions. I finished the edits and we rushed over to UN Headquarters. We made our way upstairs to the level of the Security Council. We huddled together outside the large, heavy wooden door of the Chamber. Someone asked Ron if he had the compass. He turned to face us and, without missing a beat, pointed at me and replied, "Klompas is right here!"

Mr. President,

The citizens of Israel want to live in peace. We want to see our children grow up and grow old without ever running for a bomb shelter or putting on an army uniform. I hope that some day we read about attacks on the Jewish people in history books rather than in newspapers. But that day has not yet come. For now, we are forced to wage a war against a terrorist group committed to our destruction. Night has fallen in Israel. Rather than sleeping soundly in their beds, our sons and daughters are out there in the darkness standing guard over the people of Israel. In the Book of Psalms, King David says: "Too long have I lived among those who hate peace. I am for peace; but when I speak, they are for war."

Mr. President—Israel was left with no choice. But each of you has a choice . . . The leaders of many governments represented in this room have already expressed their support for Israel's right to defend itself. We thank them for standing at our side at this important hour. I ask the rest of you to join them.

I have with me a compass. I offer it to the international community in the hopes that it will guide you toward making the right decision. Stand for moral clarity, stand for good against evil, and stand for right against wrong."

[EXCERPT OF AMBASSADOR PROSOR'S SPEECH
TO THE SECURITY COUNCIL ON JULY 18, 2014]

Just as one speech wrapped up, I had to immediately get started on the next one. The Security Council could call an emergency session and I would have just a few hours to prepare remarks and get to the Council.

One Sunday, I was working at Ella's apartment in Brooklyn, preparing for a speech scheduled to be delivered on Tuesday. Around lunchtime, Simonne came by to help. She had been negotiating a resolution on Sustainable Development Goals at the United Nations for forty straight hours. Despite her utter exhaustion, she offered to give us a hand, and we were grateful for the help.

At 6 p.m., we got a call to say there was going to be an emergency session and we had to get to the office immediately. With a sinking feeling, I looked down at my clothes. I was wearing capris and a ratty old t-shirt, certainly nothing I could wear in the Security Council. I was going to have to go home first, and home was over an hour away through Manhattan traffic.

I turned to Simonne and said, "Do you have your car here?"

With red rimmed eyes, she stared at me silently before slowly and suspiciously answering, "Yes."

"I know you're exhausted, but is there any chance you can drive me home and then drive me to the office?"

Ella interjected, "There isn't time. You have to write the speech."

I replied, "I have my laptop, I'll write it in the car."

Simonne picked up her keys and we rushed outside. I balanced the laptop on my knees as Simonne typed my address into her phone's GPS. I grabbed my phone and called my speechwriting predecessor, Nate.

Holding the phone in the crook of my neck, while typing, I said, "Nate, I need your help."

"What's going on?" he asked.

"We have an emergency Security Council session starting soon," I continued, "Can you write the introduction and conclusion for me while I work on the body?"

Without hesitating he offered, "I'll do it. What am I writing?"

With a huge sigh, I asked him to convey that Israel didn't ask for this conflict. That we had accepted every cease-fire put on the table, and that Hamas—and Hamas alone—was prolonging the conflict. I hung up the phone and turned back to my computer as Simonne weaved through New York traffic.

I typed furiously, but soon discovered I get extremely nauseated typing in a moving car. Blinking hard and taking deep breaths, Simonne was so tired she was leaning forward with her chin practically touching the top of the staring wheel and fighting to keep her eyes wide open.

"You OK?" I asked.

"I am so tired."

I surveyed Simonne. She was wearing yoga pants and a tank top, her hair was frazzled, and she was pale with dark circles around her eyes. I was certain I didn't look much better.

I continued typing, trying hard not to look at the screen to ward off the growing nausea. When we arrived at my apartment, I ran inside, pulled on a suit, grabbed some candy bars to energize Simonne, and ran back outside to the car.

As we drove downtown, Nate called to say he had written the introduction and was working on the conclusion. I opened his email on my phone and saw it was great. Simonne dropped me off in front of the office and went to find a parking spot. As I got off the elevator, I was met by one of the staff who told me Ron would not be delivering a speech after all. We would all attend the Security Council meeting and then he would speak to the media.

I went to my computer and typed up a statement. Ella and I took it to Ron and he hated it. He rattled off a list of instructions and sent me back to my office to start over. As I got back to my desk, we got a call saying Ron had to leave immediately to deliver the statement. I typed as fast as I could while Ella paced in front of me. Ron was waiting in the car downstairs for us. I finished typing his notes, hit print, grabbed the papers off the printer— checked they were the correct version—and we ran down to the car. We hurried into the UN complex to the media stakeout area and Ron stepped to the podium to deliver his remarks.

———————

The next day, I resumed work on the quarterly Middle East debate that was to take place on Tuesday. The Secretary-General had announced he would fly to the Middle East to meet with leaders to try and forge a lasting ceasefire. Protocol directed Ron fly with him, which meant our deputy ambassador would deliver the speech. I worked all day to finalize the remarks and sat with him late in the day to listen to him read it aloud a few times.

The following morning, members of the Israeli delegation arrived at the Security Council and took our seats. In our first speech to the Council, Ron had sounded a siren. In his second, he came with a compass and accused the international community of losing its moral compass. I should have expected that the Palestinians would, by this point, come armed with their own props. I looked across the room and saw members of the Palestinian delegation were wearing black ribbons and keffiyehs, checkered black and white scarfs that had become a symbol of Palestinian nationalism. When the session started, the Palestinian ambassador delivered his remarks and held up a series of photographs of Palestinian children who had died in Gaza.

Ella was back in the office watching on the live webcast. She sent me a text to say we needed to respond in some way to the photos. I scribbled a note and passed it forward to the deputy ambassador. He looked at the note and shook his head, unwilling to engage the Palestinians on this point.

Every day, the news was filled with heartbreaking photos of the death and destruction in Gaza. Just that morning, I had read a *New York Times* article telling the story of a family of fifteen in which the father split the family into groups and sent them to different rooms. If the home was hit by an Israeli shell or Hamas rocket, he hoped it would increase the chance of some family members surviving.

Israel faced impossible decisions. How do you fight an enemy that takes its own people hostage? How do you combat an enemy who hides bombs and rocket launchers in schools, hospitals, and mosques? Renowned Israeli writer Amos Oz asked this question far more eloquently, writing, "What would you do if your neighbor across the street sits down on the balcony, puts his little boy on his lap, and starts shooting machine gun fire into your nursery?"

These thoughts influenced the speech. An excerpt of the final draft read:

Mr. President,

As we speak, the Israel Defense Forces are fighting to rid Gaza of the Hamas military infrastructure that has terrorized the Israeli people and devastated the Palestinian people for well over a decade. Trust me, when I tell you— Gaza is the very last place that we want our soldiers to be.

This is not a war we chose. It was our last resort.

Hamas has sent suicide bombers into our cafes and onto our buses. It has sent armed terrorists through tunnels into our homes and schools. And it has launched over 12,000 rockets towards our towns and cities in the last 10 years.

Israel is a small country and every single person has been affected by terrorism. Israelis may have grown up with this threat in our backyard, but we have never and will never grow used to it. We will never grow used to the sound of sirens or the roar of rockets overhead. We will never grow used to seeing our children in army uniforms and we will never, ever become accustomed to burying our sons and daughters—as too many Israeli families have had to do since Hamas dragged us into this conflict.

[REMARKS TO THE SECURITY COUNCIL,
JULY 22, 2014]

As I traveled home that evening, I thought of the people affected and the terrible decisions families on both sides were being forced to make. I climbed up the stairs of the subway station and discovered it was raining. A little girl standing in a doorway turned to her mother and said, "God is crying"

The mother smiled down at the child and said, "It's just rain."

I walked past and thought perhaps the little girl knew better than the rest of us.

Ze loke'ach kefar / It takes a village

Is anybody listening?

With each passing day, pressure grew for the Security Council to impose a cease-fire. Over the weekend, there was a twelve-hour lull in fighting following intense American and UN mediation efforts, but Hamas soon resumed firing rockets at Israel. Twenty days into the war, 1,030 Palestinians had died. Israel had lost forty-three soldiers in battle, and rockets fired from Gaza killed two Israeli civilians and a Thai worker.

Early Sunday morning, I was told to prepare for an emergency Security Council session. Later that morning, I was told the session was postponed, only to later be told it was happening. This continued throughout the day until 9 p.m. when I got a phone call to come straight to the office. The Security Council would convene at midnight to read a non-binding presidential statement. Less significant than a Security Council resolution, presidential statements become part of the Council's official record and must be approved at a council meeting. I asked why the Council couldn't wait until morning and was told the Arab nations pressured the Council to take action that would coincide with the Eid al-Fitr holiday, marking the end of the holy month of Ramadan.

Speaking through third parties, both the Israelis and the Palestinians agreed not to give speeches in the Council, but it went without saying both sides would immediately exit the Council and make a beeline for the press. We met in the Council at midnight and listened to the Rwandan ambassador, Eugène-Richard Gasana, read the statement. It urged all parties "to accept and fully implement the humanitarian cease-fire," and allow for the delivery of urgently needed assistance. The statement also called on the parties "to engage in efforts to achieve a durable and fully respected cease-fire, based on the Egyptian initiative." His statement made no mention of Hamas or the rockets being fired at Israeli citizens.

When the Council session concluded, Ron, Ella, and I stepped out of the formal Chamber and waited in the Quiet Room, an antechamber abutting the Security Council. The room was outfitted with comfortable chairs and a huge television showing a live stream of the Palestinian ambassador speaking to the press just outside the Quiet Room.

While we waited, American ambassador Samantha Power walked into the room and Ron went to speak quietly with her. He spread out a series of maps, pointing out locations where Hamas was firing rockets from schools and civilian structures. The maps also showed the locations where Hamas's dozen terror tunnels emerged inside Israel, often inside Israeli communities.

He described the tunnels in detail explaining they weren't simple, shallow burrows. In Gaza, there is a city above ground and a city below ground. Below the Strip are miles of dense terror tunnels crisscrossing like a giant web. Reinforced with thousands of tons of concrete and supported by massive beams, Hamas had constructed a vast underground terror network. Many of the tunnels were equipped with electricity and contained enough provisions to allow its occupants to live underground for several months. Many were used to store weapons and explosives and one even held a fleet of motorcycles. During the conflict, dozens of heavily armed terrorists used the tunnels to infiltrate Israel. They emerged with automatic weapons, wearing

Israeli military uniforms, and carrying tranquilizers and handcuffs, on a mission to kidnap and kill Israelis.

When Ron finished speaking with Power, he stepped out of the room to talk to the press. At two o'clock in the morning, our delegation finally exited the UN complex. When we got outside, I looked up at the dark sky and thought about the new day that was starting in Israel and wondered how much longer the war would last.

Five hours later, we were back in the office. Ron had a series of television interviews and I needed to update our messages with instructions from Jerusalem. I was sitting in Ron's office with some of the other staff, chatting and scrolling through my Twitter feed. I stopped on a post showing me that just down the street thousands of people had gathered outside the United Nations for a New York Stands with Israel rally.

I read the tweet out loud, looked up at Ron, and said, "You should go."

The room went silent.

He looked at me and said, "Yeah?"

"Why not?" I continued. "Let's go out there."

"OK, let's do it," and he stood from his chair.

The always levelheaded Dafna interjected, "Not so fast, I'll call security," and left the room to make the call.

"And I'll work on a few remarks," I said, walking around the desk and sitting at Ron's computer. In ten minutes, I had a few lines ready, and we hustled down to the car and drove the four blocks to Dag Hammarskjold Plaza in front of the United Nations. As we turned into the plaza, I was stunned to see swells of people packed together waving Israeli flags and holding signs pronouncing their solidarity with Israel. The car rolled slowly behind the stage. As we stepped out into the hot July sunshine, we were met with a deafening surge of applause. I surveyed the crowd, felt the charge in the air, and felt proud to be standing at Ron's side. He sprung onto the stage and the crowd erupted in cheers.

Ladies and Gentlemen,

What can I tell you? Seeing you here united for Israel before the United Nations is absolutely amazing. Your voice should echo throughout the halls of the United Nations, into the international community, saying the following: Kol Yisrael arevim zeh lazeh, Yisrael arevim zeh bazeh.

All of Israel are responsible for one another. Israel wants peace but there cannot be peace if Hamas keeps on digging terror tunnels . . . [and] sending missiles indiscriminately into civilian populations . . . We are defending our own citizens for something we all cherish—that is the sanctity of life.

We reach out to everyone who wants peace with us, but we will hold the Shield of David very close to our chest, because only a very strong Israel can achieve peace in this region. Thank you very much—thank you for standing up united for Israel before the United Nations.

[EXCERPT OF SPEECH TO NEW YORK STANDS
WITH ISRAEL RALLY ON JULY 28, 2014]

When Ron finished speaking, we made our way back to the car and set off for an interview across town at CBS. For the rest of the day, we traveled between news stations. Late in the afternoon, I climbed into the car and checked my fitness tracker. It showed I had gotten an average of three hours and twenty minutes sleep each night over the past week. I leaned my head back in the car and tried to rest, but too many thoughts nagged at me.

When I returned to the office, I went to find a diplomat who had been sending me increasingly urgent messages all day. He needed help writing a letter responding to a UN Human Rights Council resolution calling for an investigation of Israel's alleged war crimes. We sat together to prepare the letter and went to Ron's office to have it reviewed. As Ron read through, he grew unexpectedly angry and eventually exploded, "They are accusing us of the worst crimes imaginable and this is what you're going to write to them? This doesn't begin to respond to them. I want to shove it to these people." He balled up the letter and sent us out of the room to write something new.

In late July, the UN Human Rights Council convened a special session to address the escalating violence between Israelis and Palestinians in Gaza.* Members of the Council voted to appoint a commission of inquiry to investigate alleged violations of international humanitarian laws. At the time, the Council included notorious human rights abusers China, Russia, Saudi Arabia, and the United Arab Emirates. The Council adopted resolution S-21/1 which, "Strongly condemns the failure of Israel, the occupying Power, to end its prolonged occupation of the Occupied Palestinian Territory, including East Jerusalem, in accordance with international law and relevant United Nations resolutions." The resolution went on to say the Council "condemns in the strongest terms the widespread, systematic and gross violations of international human rights and fundamental freedoms arising from the Israeli military operations carried out in the Occupied Palestinian Territory since 13 June 2014, particularly the latest Israeli military assault on the occupied Gaza Strip, by air, land and sea."

There were 1,725 words in the resolution, and not one mention of Hamas. There was also no mention of the thousands of rockets fired by terrorists or the tunnels that Hamas was using to infiltrate and attack Israel. It was clear

---

* http://www.ohchr.org/EN/HRBodies/HRC/SpecialSessions/Session21/Pages/21stSpecialSession.aspx

from the text the Council had already judged Israel and found it guilty. The resolution passed by a vote of 29 to 1, with only the United States opposing the commission of inquiry. In her remarks to the National Jewish Leaders Assembly a week later, National Security Advisor Susan Rice said:

No country is immune to criticism—nor should it be. But when that criticism takes the form of singling out just one country unfairly, bitterly, and relentlessly—over and over and over—that's just wrong, and we all know it.

I saw this firsthand during my years at the United Nations, where America always has Israel's back when its basic right of self-defense is challenged. Believe me, I remember all too well the fight against the deeply flawed Goldstone Report. So, last week, when the United Nations Human Rights Council again passed a one-sided resolution calling for a commission of inquiry that will have no positive impact and should never have been created— the United States stood with Israel and said "No!" We were the lone vote in the Human Rights Council. Even our closest friends on the Council abstained. It was 29-1. But the "1," as usual, was America. That's what we mean when we say, "You are not alone."

We take that stand on principle. It's important not just for Israel, but for the credibility of the United Nations itself. The U.N. does exceptional, lifesaving things around the world: empowering women and girls, keeping the peace in far-flung conflict zones, providing humanitarian aid whether in Gaza, Syria, or Congo and around the world. The world needs the United Nations. So when countries single out Israel for unfair treatment at the U.N., it isn't just a problem for Israel. It's a problem for all of us.

[NATIONAL SECURITY ADVISOR SUSAN E. RICE,

JULY 28, 2014]

Two weeks later, the Council appointed William Schabas, a Canadian international law expert, to lead a three-member group investigating alleged war crimes from the military offensive in Gaza. Even by UN standards, it was an appalling choice. Schabas is an outspoken critic of Israel* who is on record calling for the prosecution of Prime Minister Netanyahu and former President Shimon Peres, saying, "My favorite would be Netanyahu within the dock of the International Criminal Court."† In the midst of the conflict on July 17, 2014, Schabas told the BBC, "There are huge numbers of civilian casualties on one side and virtually no civilian causalities on the other, and so prima facie, there is evidence of disproportionality in the response that Israel is undertaking in order to protect itself."

Within six months, the evidence of his bias became overwhelming and Schabas was forced to resign when it was revealed that, in 2012, he had been paid to do legal work for the Palestine Liberation Organization.

———————

On top of writing untold numbers of speeches, letters, and media messages relating to Operation Protective Edge, we were contacted by the *New York Times* and asked to submit an op-ed. I discussed ideas with Ron and he decided to offer an article describing how Israel has been forced to confront the moral dilemmas that go hand-in-hand with combating terrorism, long before the rest of the world has awakened to the threat. Delighted at the prospect of having Ron featured in the *Times* and ignoring the pesky detail of the inordinate time and effort that went into writing an op-ed for a prestigious newspaper, Anat promised the editor a first draft by morning. I was

———————

* http://mfa.gov.il/MFA/ForeignPolicy/Issues/Pages/The-Human-Rights-Council
-commission-of-inquiry-on-Gaza.aspx
† Timestamp: 12:29, https://www.youtube.com/watch?v=Vm_WhxIGytk&feature
=youtu.be&t=12m29s

dumbfounded when she told me, and I fumed when she took off for the evening and left me at my desk to work on the piece. I sat down at my desk and started at my cursor blinking on the blank screen. It was going to be a long, sleepless night ahead. I put my head in my hands and gave myself sixty seconds to wallow in self-pity, before sitting up and calling in reinforcements.

First, I emailed Ella asking for ideas and then shot off an email to Avishai asking if he had some time to brainstorm. A minute later my phone rang. It was Avishai, ready to help. I explained Ron's thoughts and we threw around ideas. While I was on the phone, Ella wrote back and suggested we start the article with one of Ron's favorite anecdotes about how Israel was one of the first countries to implement strict security measures in airports, because Israel has long had to stay one step ahead of terrorism.

Avishai and I worked on an outline and he offered to write up the first half of the piece. The man is a saint. Together we wrote the article and sent it off to Ron. In the morning, I got Ron's edits and sent the article to Anat to pitch. The *New York Times* turned down the article, so we gave it to an editor at the *New York Post* who promptly published the piece.

In 1968, three members of the Popular Front for the Liberation of Palestine hijacked an Israel-bound El Al flight, diverting it to Algiers. It was one of the first terrorist hijackings in modern history.

In response, Israel implemented a wave of unprecedented airport security reforms —including luggage checks and individual passenger screenings.

For its efforts to protect passengers, Israel was scorned by the liberal elite for putting innocent travelers through an invasive and burdensome ordeal.

Thirty-three years later, al Qaeda terrorists hijacked four US planes, crashing two into the World Trade Center. Today, Israel's once-"insensitive" policies have become the standard procedure in every airport across the globe.

[EXCERPT FROM "ISRAEL'S FIGHT TODAY WILL BE
YOURS TOMORROW" PUBLISHED IN THE
NEW YORK POST ON JULY 31, 2014].

———————

On Friday, August 1, two hours after Hamas agreed to a cease-fire, terrorists ambushed three Israeli soldiers from a tunnel located in the basement of a house in Gaza. Two of the soldiers were killed and the third, twenty-three-year-old Hadar Goldin, was shot and dragged into a tunnel to kidnap him. It was the second time a soldier had been presumed to be captured in Gaza. The news broke my heart. When Israelis hear a soldier has come to harm, he or she immediately becomes everyone's son or daughter.

I arrived at work that morning and Simonne arrived a short while later frantic and crying. Oblivious to those around her, she kept uttering, "Oh no, oh no, oh no." Ella and Dafna followed closely behind her. Quietly, Ella explained that the missing soldier was her sister's brother-in-law. I felt my stomach sink. Simonne was frantically trying to call her family in Israel to get information, but the line was busy. We waited anxiously at her side until she got through to her sister who confirmed the family had been notified that Hadar was missing in Gaza and presumed kidnapped by Hamas. Time moved in slow motion as Simonne collapsed into sobs. We hugged her, at a loss for reassuring words.

Simonne refused to go home and spent the next few hours calling her family and trying to decide whether she should get on a plane and fly to Israel. All of us spent the day anxiously checking for updates on Hadar's whereabouts. Images of Hadar started appearing online. It was devastating to look at photos of the handsome, smiling young man. That night, I lit an extra Shabbat candle and prayed he would return home safely. The following day we learned the army had pronounced Hadar killed in action.

To this day, Hamas continues to hold Hadar's body, presumably as a bargaining chip to extract political or military concessions from Israel. The terror group is also holding the remains of Oron Shaul, another soldier killed in Operation Protective Edge.

On Monday morning, word circulated that the General Assembly planned to hold a session Wednesday to address the conflict between Israel and Hamas. After weeks of having mere hours to write a speech, two full days seemed like a luxury.

I finished the speech Monday afternoon and took it to Ron early Tuesday. He had asked me to include fresh language and creative new ideas, but as he read through the speech he evoked sections from previous speeches and instructed me to insert them, "word for word." Throughout the day, I brought him drafts, and he requested revisions, additions, and more material. What began as five-minute remarks was quickly ballooning into an unwieldy oration. That evening, I sent the speech to Ron and called to get his feedback. He read the speech over the phone and when he reached the end, paused and said to me, "I really don't like it. I think you should start again."

Exasperated, I said, "I've been working on this speech for eleven hours. You've been looking at drafts all day, and now you want a new one? What do you want it to say?" He told me he would think about it and get back to me. Experience had long since taught me that he would call back sometime between five minutes later and never. I spun around to the window and watched as the sky grew dark outside. I knew I would be writing a new speech but needed to spend a little time in denial.

Eventually I gave in and, realizing I needed fresh eyes and ideas, called Yonatan, our diplomat to the United Nations' Fifth Committee and backup spokesman. He was out with friends, but promptly offered to return to the office. Thirty minutes later he stepped into my office somewhat tipsy, but ready to work. Ella had gone home earlier in the day with food poisoning. I called, and she offered to stay on the line and talk through ideas, but we gave up on that idea when she had to drop the phone and rush to the toilet to throw up.

With Yonatan pacing back and forth offering ideas and suggestions, I rewrote the speech, weaving in the ideas Ron had given me earlier in the day. The following morning, I sat with Ron in his office and reviewed the speech. Finally satisfied, we trotted down to the car for the short drive to the United Nations. We made our way to the Trusteeship Council where the debate was being held. We were late—naturally—but hadn't missed much. For the next hour, a parade of UN officials accused Israel of committing a lengthy list of grievous crimes. Ron shook his head as the Secretary-General said, "The fighting has raised serious questions about respect for the principles of distinction and proportionality in international humanitarian law."

The most striking part of the session were the many topics acutely avoided by UN officials. There was no mention of Hamas or terrorists using Palestinians civilians as human shields, or the terror group violating eight cease-fire agreements. There was just a passing mention of the 3,500 rockets fired at Israel and the terror tunnels that ran from the Gaza Strip into the heart of Israeli communities. The failure to condemn attacks against Israeli civilians betrayed a clear bias. No institution can purport to champion human rights if it can't demonstrate it cares equally about the dignity, well-being, and safety of *all* people, Israelis included.

Ron grew angry as he listened to the lengthy one-sided diatribes. He reached for a pen and furiously wrote in the margins of his speech. When it came time for him to speak, he delivered the introduction of his written remarks and then put down his papers, looked up, and continued:

I heard the head of UNRWA speaking today, and the special envoy, and the briefings of other high U.N. officials this morning. They talked about addressing the causes and consequences of this conflict.

So, let's begin by reminding this Assembly of something. When I headed Israel's Foreign Service in 2005, Israel turned every inch of Gaza to the Palestinians. We hoped that this would serve as a model for two societies to live side by side in peace. But instead, Hamas built a terror stronghold.

We went completely out of Gaza. We left them greenhouses. Gaza could have turned into an amazing place. Does Israel have an interest in Gaza? We left never to turn back into Gaza. But look at what Hamas created in Gaza.

And I never heard a clear and unequivocal statement by the officials of the United Nations saying squarely and unequivocally that all attempts to achieve a cease-fire were broken by Hamas. Israel said yes to each and every one of them, Hamas said no. You know it's possible to utter that statement.

And, yes, you say the nice sentence that "Israel has legitimate security needs that must be addressed." Very nice words. But how do you address these needs, how do you defend your citizens when Hamas uses the money that come from good people in this assembly to build Gaza, to build terror tunnels, hundreds of millions, cement, steel, instead of building kindergartens and schools and hospitals? Creating a launching pad for nearly 10,000 missiles? You ask yourself, my god, in that small place, how could they

amass that many rockets in one place? Those are the consequences? We went
out of Gaza because we wanted that to be a model for the next stage.

[EXCERPT OF AMBASSADOR PROSOR'S SPEECH
TO THE GENERAL ASSEMBLY ON AUGUST 6, 2014]

I looked around the room to see if his words were resonating with the audience of diplomats. While it was clear they were listening, they gave no indication of whether they agreed. When he finished getting all his thoughts off his chest, Ron picked up his speech and continued reading.

Mr. President,

Israel did everything in its power to avoid this conflict. We accepted
every cease-fire—even as the people of Israel came under attack. The
world witnessed Hamas's understanding of "cease-fires"—Israel ceases and
Hamas fires.

We were left with no choice. We sent our sons and daughters into Gaza for
one reason and one reason only—to restore sustained quiet in Israel and
disrupt the Hamas infrastructure that has produced terror and violence for
well over a decade.

Israel deeply regrets the loss of innocent lives. We are heartbroken by the
stories and images of loss and grief that have emerged from Gaza. To us, the
death of any civilian—Israeli or Palestinian—is a tragedy.

But Israel faces an enemy that does not abide by any rules or morals. Hamas
sees no problem with abusing international humanitarian centers and religious institutions for terrorist purposes. It stores weapons in UN facilities,

transports terrorists in ambulances, and fires rockets indiscriminately from
mosques, schools, and hospitals deep into the heart of civilian centers.

[EXCERPT OF AMBASSADOR PROSOR'S SPEECH
TO THE GENERAL ASSEMBLY ON AUGUST 6, 2014]

I returned to the office and was typing up the adlib section of the speech
when a colleague appeared in my doorway. "Channel 2 carried the speech
live in Israel. They're proud we're telling the world our side of the story."
Clearly pleased, he retreated down the hall and I turned back to my
computer.

A few days later, Ron was challenged by Peter Lerner, the IDF's then-
spokesman and head of its Foreign Press Branch, to participate in the ALS
Ice Bucket Challenge. During the summer of 2014, you couldn't scroll
through a social media site without seeing everyone from Bill Gates to Bill
Clinton to Bon Jovi taking up the challenge. As soon as the dare was issued,
a few of us piled into a taxi and headed over to Ron's residence. There was
no chance we would pass on an opportunity to dump ice on our boss's head.
In the car, we discussed what Ron should say in the video and who he should
challenge. We arrived at his apartment, dug out a bucket, and filled it with
water. I opened Ron's freezer and grabbed all the ice I could find.

Ron watched sceptically and asked, "Do you really need all of it?"

"Absolutely," I replied, unable to conceal a huge grin.

We went outside, and Ron practiced what he would say on camera. A
small crowd of New Yorkers gathered on the sidewalk to watch. Ron looked
around and noted the broad smiles on the faces of his staff. He shook his
head and instructed me to start videoing. The lighthearted afternoon came

to a halt shortly after we finished the video,* checked our phones, and learned Hamas had broken the latest cease-fire. Fun over, we piled into the car and headed to the office.

The fighting continued for another week until August 26 when an open-ended cease-fire was reached. It was the eleventh ceasefire Israel had agreed to accept. Over the previous fifty days, seventy people were killed on the Israeli side.† The death toll included sixty-four soldiers and six Israeli civilians killed by rockets or mortars fired from Gaza. The youngest victim was four-year-old Daniel Tregerman. He was playing in his family's living room when a mortar struck his house.

Gaza health officials reported that more than 2,100 Palestinians were killed in Gaza and about half were believed to be civilians. Many thousands more were wounded. Throughout the conflict, the media focused on the uneven death tolls, and Israel was roundly criticized for responding "disproportionately."

Proportionality in warfare is not a numbers game. Rather, proportionality means using sufficient, but not excessive, force to accomplish a military objective. If Israel had listened to the critics who accused it of employing disproportionate force, there would have been two choices. Either it could have ended its military offensive after seventy Palestinians were killed (the number of Israelis killed), and allowed Hamas to continue to attack. Or it could have dismantled its Iron Dome defense system and allowed thousands of Israeli citizens to be killed for the sake of arithmetic equivalency. Both choices are

---

* https://www.youtube.com/watch?v=AF4kPd0l-w8.
† https://www.jpost.com/Operation-Protective-Edge/50-days-of-Israels-Gaza -operation-Protective-Edge-by-the-numbers-372574

illogical, but when it comes to the media's coverage of Israel, logic isn't in play. Hamas understands that and exploits the Western media's obsessive focus on proportionality by operating its command centers in hospitals, launching rockets from schoolyards, and building tunnels under mosques.

During Operation Protective Edge, the IDF struck some 5,226 targets in Gaza, including 1,814 targets linked to rocket firings, 109 weapons depots, and eighty-five weapon-making facilities. The Air Force also carried out 840 strikes to support ground forces, and 192 attacks on Hamas military or training sites. Israeli military and intelligence sources reported they found and destroyed thirty-two tunnels within Gaza, fourteen of which snaked into Israel.

Reports would later surface that Hamas had intended to use its tunnel network to launch a major attack on the Jewish New Year, Rosh Hashanah. According to former IDF Spokesman Lt. Col. Peter Lerner, "Hamas had a plan. A simultaneous, coordinated, surprise attack within Israel. They planned to send two hundred terrorists armed to the teeth toward civilian populations. This was going to be a coordinated attack. The concept of operations involved fourteen offensive tunnels into Israel. With at least ten men in each tunnel, they would infiltrate and inflict mass casualties."*

The kidnapping and murder of the three Israeli boys had set things in motion before Hamas was ready for its offensive. The early discovery of these tunnels likely prevented a massive terror attack.

The days and weeks of Operation Protective Edge were the most physically and emotionally challenging of my life and I was badly in need of a rest. The day the war ended, I booked a flight to California and spent a week sitting on a beach. I sent Ella a photo of the picturesque scene before me and she sent back a text saying, "Rest up, the new session of the General Assembly is just around the corner."

---

* Adam Ciralsky, "Did Israel Avert a Hamas Massacre?" *Vanity Fair*, October 21, 2014, http://www.vanityfair.com/politics/2014/10/gaza-tunnel-plot-israeli-intelligence

CHAPTER 13

La'asot chaim / Have fun

What do you get a president who has everything?

I returned from California rested and ready for the long hours and frenzied chaos of another General Assembly session. My first day back in the office, I was delighted to discover a new batch of interns had joined the Mission, and someone even had the bright idea of streamlining the process by having them all start on the same day. They even arranged an orientation to prepare the interns for their new roles.

I asked Keinan about all these new wonders of organizational management, and he proudly answered, "We're making the process as un-Israeli as possible." It seemed like a great leap forward until I went looking for my new intern and learned he would be in orientation all week, and therefore unavailable to assist me.

Shortly before the General Assembly began, David Frum, political commentator and former speechwriter for President George W. Bush, approached the Mission about shadowing Ron for a day and running a profile piece on the Mission's work in the *Atlantic*. Our spokesperson arranged for him to accompany us on a particularly eventful day. Ron was scheduled to deliver three speeches in the United Nations—one on the Responsibility to Protect doctrine, the second at a Security Council debate on children in armed conflict, and a third on the rise in anti-Semitism.

Since the summer conflict with Hamas in Gaza, there had been an alarming rise in global anti-Semitism. The World Zionist Organization released a reporting showing a 400-percent rise in anti-Semitic incidents in Europe, a 1,200 percent spike in South America, and a 127-percent rise in the United States. Our good friends at the Permanent Mission of Palau were having none of this. An archipelago of over five hundred islands in the western Pacific Ocean, Palau is one of the few nations to staunchly stand at Israel's side at the United Nations. It approached us about hosting a special session entitled "Global Anti-Semitism: A Threat to International Peace and Security."

I sat with Ron to discuss his remarks. He wanted to begin with a quote from Israeli poet Zelda Mishkovsky, "Unto every person there is a name given to him by God and given to him by his parents." Running with the idea, I wrote:

We must never lose sight of the fact that every human being is an individual—a person with feelings, thoughts, ideas and dreams. As renowned Israeli poet Zelda Mishkovsky wrote, "Unto every person there is a name given to him by God and one given to him by his parents."

And yet history has shown us that there are always those who believe that some lives are worth less than others because of their faith, their nationality, their ethnicity or even their ancestry.

From Australia to Argentina and from the United Kingdom to the United States Jews have been attacked on streets for wearing a kippah, their businesses have been vandalized, and riots have erupted outside synagogues.

These are not acceptable protests—they are the words and actions of bigots who seek to demonize a democracy and its people.

[GLOBAL ANTI-SEMITISM SPEECH,
SEPTEMBER 8, 2014]

I asked one of my new interns to come up with an idea for the body of the speech. He suggested telling the story of two Jews, one living in Europe in 1937 and the second living in Europe in 2013.

I want to share with you the story of a young mother named Anna and her 6-month old baby. The two left their home in the center of Paris on a beautiful spring morning and walked the short distance to a nearby bus station.

As they stood waiting for the bus an elderly woman walked up to Anna and yelled, "Dirty Jews. Enough with your children already" and the elderly woman began violently shaking the baby's stroller. People passed by without saying a word.

Four hundred miles away in the heart of Berlin, a 12-year-old boy named Shmuel stood at a metro terminal. As he searched through his backpack looking for a sandwich, a group of teenagers walked up and shouted, "Look! This Jew is eating our bread. Jews are stealing our food." And although the station was crowded with commuters, no one said or did a thing.

The attack on Shmuel took place in 1937 while the attack on Anna took place two months ago. Seventy-seven years may have passed, yet it seems there is little difference for a European Jew in 1937 and in 2014.

There are countless Jews—all with a name, a family, and a story—who have found themselves under attack in recent weeks.

Anti-Semitic rhetoric morphed into violence and led to the firebombing of a synagogue in Wuppertal, Germany, earlier this month. It reminded me of the first torching of a synagogue that took place during the Nazi pogroms in 1938.

Where is the outrage? Where are the universal calls of condemnation? My friends—the silence of 2014 sounds exactly like the silence of the 1930s."

[Global Anti-Semitism speech,
September 8, 2014]

On September 8, Ron, Anat, journalist Frum, and I made our way to the UN complex. We weaved through the corridors and made our way to the anti-Semitism event. The timing was tight between when Ron was scheduled to deliver remarks at the anti-Semitism event and his remarks in the Security Council. As soon as he finished his first speech, Anat ushered our little group out of the Trusteeship Council and across the plush carpeted corridors to the Security Council.

Ron and Frum slid into seats in the front row of the Council chamber and I went to hand copies of Ron's speech to the interpreters. The Security Council session was held in response to the targeting of children by extremist armed groups like ISIS and Boko Haram. Earlier in the year, Boko Haram had become a household name after abducting over two hundred girls from a boarding school in the northern Nigerian town of Chibok.

When it was Ron's turn to speak, he strode to the Council's polished horseshoe-shaped table and took his place in the pale blue leather chair. I took the seat behind him and Ella relinquished her spot so Frum could sit with us at the Council table. It took a minute before I realized that seated beside Ron was Forrest Whitaker, the Academy award-winning actor and a UN Special Envoy for Peace and Reconciliation.

A lot of work had gone into preparing Ron's Security Council speech. Given the recent war with Hamas in Gaza, there was no doubt that some member states would use the Council's debate on children in armed conflict to condemn Israel for the deaths of Palestinian children. Ron's speech was going to have to address these accusations. Moreover, I wanted to address the impact of Hamas's terror on Israeli children. I had thought for days about how to make the remarks memorable and finally found inspiration from one of the most famous children's authors of all time, Dr. Seuss.

> One of the world's most-beloved children's authors, Dr. Seuss, once wrote: "A person's a person, no matter how small." All children around the world deserve to grow up in an environment where their dignity and human rights are respected and their aspirations are valued. Yet in too many parts of the world, children are the targets of violence and the casualties of conflict . . .

> In the Middle East, terrorists regularly single out children in their attacks. In June, millions of Israelis were numb with horror when they learned that Hamas terrorists kidnapped and murdered three Israeli teenagers—Eyal, Gilad and Naftali—as they made their way home from school.

> This is just one of many attacks targeting Israeli children. Over the summer, over 3,800 rockets and mortars were fired into Israel—an average of one rocket every ten minutes. These rockets landed on Israeli kindergartens, playgrounds, and homes. Four-year-old Daniel Tregerman of Kibbutz Nahal Oz was one of the tragic casualties of these rockets."

> [CHILDREN IN ARMED CONFLICT,
> SEPTEMBER 8, 2014]

Pleased with the speech, I walked out of the Security Council alongside Frum and asked what he thought of Ron's remarks. His answer: "It wasn't as sleepy as I expected." It was good of him to keep my ego in check.

Between delivering speeches, Ron met with Yonatan, who was leading Israel's campaign to make Yom Kippur an official UN holiday. The global body observes ten holidays. Six reflect the fact the institution is based in New York and the city grinds to a halt on major American holidays: New Year's Day, Presidents' Day, Memorial Day, Independence Day, Labor Day, and Thanksgiving. Four others are major religious festivals: the Christian holy days of Good Friday and Christmas, and the Muslim holy days of Eid al-Fitr and Eid al-Adha. Since arriving at the United Nations in 2011, one of Ron's goals was to see the body also recognize a Jewish holiday.

The United States, Australia, Canada, most EU member states, and other liberal democracies were in favor of the addition of Yom Kippur as an official addition to the UN calendar, but other member states resisted the notion. There's no one quite as vaguely creative as a diplomat unwilling to support a motion.

"It isn't the right time."

"There are more pressing matters to attend to."

"What will all the other religions think?"

"We may offend the Buddhists!"

Yonatan was engaged in full-day negotiations, wrestling with endless amorphous claims. From time to time, he would slip out of the room to update Ron on what member states were saying. Adamant this was a battle we could win, Ron bolstered Yonatan with new arguments and sent him back to the negotiations. Frum looked on and asked a few questions.

The *Atlantic* article Frum wrote came out in late September. The accompanying photo showed Ron delivering remarks to the Security Council with Forrest Whitaker to his right looking thoughtful, and yours truly tapping away at her phone (I was live tweeting the remarks). Frum's article extensively covered the Yom Kippur resolution with nary a mention of Ron's three eloquent speeches.

———————

A week later, I was sitting in my office when my phone rang.

"Darling, I have exciting news." Dafna gushed. "You need to try to stay calm."

Too late. "What is it?" I asked eagerly.

Dafna didn't often get excited, so this had to be big. She took a breath and continued, "Shimon Peres is being honored at a dinner and Ron is going to speak. Now, I am telling you again, stay calm."

I hung up and sprinted over to Dafna's desk.

"Really?" I asked bouncing with excitement.

"I told you to stay calm," Dafna scolded. She continued, "This will have to be a special speech. Get the details and then talk to Ron about what he wants to say."

I was a great fan of President Peres. Thanks to Ron, I'd met him on a couple of occasions. Peres was warm, funny, and genuinely interested in people. Putting on a faux air of cool composure, I called the event organizers and, armed with the details, a pad of paper, pen, and an intern, I went to Ron's office.

Sitting across from him, I said, "Ron, let's talk about your speech for Shimon Peres."

Ron looked up from his computer where he was scrolling through the news. He thought for a moment, swiveled his chair around, and leaned forward over his desk.

"This has to be a totally different speech. It has to be interesting, funny, and memorable," he began.

"What do you have in mind?" I asked.

He sat back. "I don't know. Engage the brain, Klompas. Think. We need to think!"

"Well, to channel Ella, it would be good to have a prop," I said.

My intern had been listening and piped up to suggest we give him a Lonely Planet travel guide.

"To mark the end of his service, like when Israelis finish military service and then go travel the world," he explained.

"Not bad," I said, "but a book isn't very exciting."

We continued exchanging ideas and then the idea came to me; we would give President Peres a backpack.

"Yes. Let's do it," Ron said.

We spoke for a while longer and I jotted down notes as Ron told me what he wanted to say about each of the honorees. I sent the intern off to a camping store to find the perfect backpack and I headed to my office to start writing.

The following day, we brought Ron a draft of the speech and he was pleased. He finished reading and said, "You know what this needs? It needs John Lennon."

I laughed. "Are you planning to sing 'Imagine?'"

"Absolutely," he answered, wiggling his eyebrows.

My intern had found a large eye-catching orange backpack. He stuffed it full of paper so it would look full and even added a small Israeli flag as a finishing touch. Later that week, I sat with Dafna and Ella in the audience of a glitzy New York hotel, lighthearted and light-headed thanks to the open bar, and watched Ron deliver his speech to a delighted crowd.

After 67 years in Israeli public service in which you climbed to amazing heights and reached every peak of accomplishment, it is time for you to do what every other Israeli does when he finishes his national service— backpack through South America! On behalf of the Israeli Mission to the United Nations, I would like to present you with this gift (hold up the backpack) to take with you as you scale new heights—from the mountains of Machu Picchu to the jungles of the Amazon.

On your next adventure, we wish you דרך צלחה *- onwards and upwards!*
[EXCERPT OF RON PROSOR'S ADL DINNER,
SEPTEMBER 22 2014]

In September, the United Nations kicked off its sixty-eighth session of the General Assembly and the compound once again flooded with a veritable who's who of royalty, presidents, prime ministers, sheikhs, and dictators. The media speculated intensely over whether US president Barack Obama and Iranian president Hassan Rouhani would meet. The previous year, shortly after Rouhani's election, the White House had offered to arrange a brief "encounter" between the two leaders, but the Iranians declined. Instead, the two had a phone conversation which the White House touted as the first direct communication between US and Iranian presidents since the 1979 Islamic revolution. This year, the press devoted endless ink and airwaves debating if Obama and Rouhani would shake hands, hold a private meeting, or "bump" into one another in the corridors.

Most media outlets didn't concern their readers with the fact that Supreme Leader Ayatollah Ali Khamenei continued to lead crowds in chants of "death to America" or that Iran had arrested and was holding US citizens Pastor Saeed Abedini, former US Marine Amir Hekmati, and *Washington Post* reporter Jason Rezaian on trumped-up charges of espionage.

As the Obama-Rouhani speculation reached fever pitch, a colleague in the Israeli Consulate called and offered a spare ticket to hear the Iranian president speak at a New York venue. I figured it would be interesting and went to Israel-the-diplomat to ask what he thought of the idea. Stooped over his computer and partially hidden behind the teetering piles of paper on his desk, he barely looked up as he answered, "Bad idea."

"Why?" I asked, surprised.

"They'll take down the names of everyone who goes to hear him speak." He continued, "I think its best that you don't end up on an Iranian intelligence services list." With that he turned back to his computer.

Yet another example of the sound career advice I never got working for the Canadians.

Reluctantly, I declined the ticket and instead walked over to the General Assembly. During the year, I often visited the iconic hall to hear Ron deliver speeches. Usually, the massive room was largely empty as delegates arrived to give a speech and then left. During high-level week the United Nations is bursting at the seams. That day, I heard speeches from the French and Egyptian presidents, the Jordanian king, and the British prime minister. Walking through the corridors, I passed President Obama, Secretary of State John Kerry, and former UK prime minister Tony Blair. It was terribly exciting to come around the corner and bump into someone I recognized from the pages of the *Economist*. I was like a kid in a candy store, albeit a candy store crowded with stern security officials tasked with preventing the giddy masses from attempting selfies with world leaders.

Having learned my lesson the previous year, I stocked my fridge with microwaveable meals, cleared my personal schedule, and prepared to spend my days and nights shuttling between the office, receptions, and the hotels of the Israeli ministers and diplomats who arrived in New York to attend the General Assembly.

On Sunday afternoon, I arrived at a small, private lunch held by the American Jewish Committee to thank our Small Island Pacific State champions, the Marshall Islands, Palau, and the Federated States of Micronesia, for their unwavering support. Just as I sat down to enjoy a carefully selected assortment of sushi and fruit, my phone pinged with a message. I needed to get to the hotel to help the visiting deputy minister of Foreign Affairs, with an upcoming speech. I grabbed a few cookies from the dessert table and headed off to his hotel a few blocks away.

Sitting in a crowded hotel boardroom, I once again marveled at the *kibbutz*-style approach to speechwriting, in which everyone felt the need to contribute. Half a dozen staff sat with the deputy minister and offered their two shekels on every line. I jotted down the suggestions and promised to send a draft later in the day. Back in my office, I read through the confusing and contradictory list of instructions from the meeting. I had learned a lot in my time working with Israelis. When I first started, I would spend hours trying to satisfy every suggestion and idea. Now wiser and far, far wearier, I crossed out the more ludicrous and perplexing proposals, and got to work making the remaining edits. An hour later, I emailed the updated draft to a member of the deputy minister's staff.

The following day, I got a call requesting a few minor changes. I printed off fresh copies and walked over to the hotel for a final review. I sat with the deputy minister and one of his advisors and listened as he read the speech. When he was satisfied, I returned to the office to work on the dozens of speeches the various diplomats would need for the fall. My phone rang, but I didn't recognize the number. I answered and the heavily accented Israeli voice on the other end skipped over the pleasantries that usually begin a phone conversation, and asked, "How do you pronounce 'lengths?' Is the g silent?"

Love these guys. I said the word a few times and the mysterious Israeli voice repeated after me.

"We can switch lengths for another word that would be easier."

"No, no. He will say it." The voice insisted. "Just tell me again how it should sound."

"Lengths."

"Len-s," came the response.

"Lengths," I repeated.

"Lenn-thes."

We played this game for a while until I was convinced he would never pronounce the word correctly. Deciding I didn't want to spend the rest of my life trapped in this conversation, I cheered and told him he had mastered the word. Without so much as a thank you or goodbye, he hung up and the call was over.

On September 29, Prime Minister Netanyahu arrived at the United Nations to speak before the global body. A few days earlier, Palestinian Authority president Mahmoud Abbas had delivered remarks in which he accused Israel of committing a "war of genocide" in the Gaza Strip. Before boarding his flight to New York, Netanyahu told reporters, "In my address to the UN General Assembly, I will refute all of the lies being directed at us and I will tell the truth about our state and about the heroic soldiers of the IDF, the most moral army in the world."*

The speech was ostensibly a response to the myriad criticisms from Israel's summer war with Hamas in Gaza. The prime minister came out swinging. He stood before the world body and announced he had come from Jerusalem to speak on behalf of the Israeli people and to, "expose the brazen lies spoken from this very podium against my country and the brave soldiers who defend it."

Picking up steam, Prime Minister Netanyahu explained that Israel's fight against Hamas was part of the larger global fight against militant Islam. "When it comes to its ultimate goals, Hamas is ISIS, and ISIS is Hamas," he declared.

Drawing an allusion to the Holocaust, he continued, "The Nazis believed in a master race, militant Islamists believe in a master faith; they just disagree on who will be the master of the master faith. The question before

----

* Spencer Ho, "Netanyahu vows to 'refute lies' in United Nations address," *Times of Israel*, September 28, 2014. https://www.timesofisrael.com/netanyahu-vows-to-repel-lies-in-un-speech/.

us is whether militant Islam will have the power to realize its violent ambitions."

A great proponent of speech props, Prime Minister Netanyahu held up a photograph taken by a French news photographer. The photo showed a rocket launcher in the foreground with children playing nearby. In his deep, booming voice, the prime minister declared, "Ladies and gentlemen, this is a war crime, and I say to President Abbas these are the crimes, the war crimes committed by your Hamas partners in the national unity government you created and for which you are responsible."

Turning smoothly to Iran, the prime minister warned of the smooth-talking charm offensive of Iran's president and foreign minister. He accused the Iranian regime of playing games to "bamboozle its way to an agreement that will leave it with thousands of centrifuges. The world's most dangerous regime will obtain the world's most dangerous weapons."

His message was clear: Iran would say or do anything to become a nuclear-armed state while getting the sanctions lifted. Turning to the topic *du jour*, ISIS, Prime Minister Netanyahu proclaimed, "To disarm ISIS but leave Iran with the bomb would be to win the battle but lose the war."

Netanyahu was a master of prose and the epitome of everything Ron wanted in his own speeches. Props! Soaring rhetoric! Graceful pivots from ISIS to Hamas to Abbas to Iran and back to ISIS! When the prime minister finished speaking, his guests and supporters in the visitor's gallery above the hall jumped to their feed and applauded loudly. Most of the country delegates on the main floor remained in their seats, staring silently ahead.

CHAPTER 14

Zazim / We're moving

How do you tell them enough is enough?

T hroughout the fall of 2014, the political situation in Israel grew increasingly tenuous. Since the end of the Gaza war in August, tensions had risen steadily in the eastern, Arab side of Jerusalem. There were almost nightly clashes between Israeli security forces and Palestinian protesters throwing rocks and firebombs.

At the heart of the violence was a battle over the Temple Mount, or as Muslims refer to it, al-Haram al-Sharif (the Noble Sanctuary). The plateau in the heart of Jerusalem is holy to Jews, Christians, and Muslims. Israel captured the Old City in the 1967 Six-Day War, and in an effort to stabilize relations with its neighbors, agreed that the administration of the Dome of the Rock and the Al-Aqsa Mosque would remain with the Waqf, the Islamic religious authority. On June 19, 1967, Israel's then-foreign minister and master orator, Abba Eban, told the UN General Assembly, "Israel is resolved to give effective expression, in cooperation with the world's great religions, to the immunity and sanctity of all the Holy Places."

That status quo agreement established in 1967 remains in place today. It directs that people of all faiths can visit the Temple Mount, but only Muslims are permitted to pray on the plaza. In every speech and press encounter, Prime Minister Netanyahu reiterated Israel would not change the status quo.

He went so far as to ban ministers and members of Knesset from entering the Temple Mount, in an effort to prevent an escalation. Even so, the Palestinian leadership fueled rumors that Israel was scheming to take control of the holy site. At a conference in Ramallah, Palestinian Authority president Abbas told an incensed crowd that Israeli settlers had no right to desecrate the Temple Mount and should be prevented from visiting the site using "all means" necessary. His incendiary remarks were broadcast on official Palestinian Authority television nineteen times in three days. From the safety and luxury of his five-star accommodations in the Qatari capital of Doha, Hamas leader Khaled Mashaal accused Israel of trying to take over al-Aqsa Mosque and called on Muslims to "defend" their holy site. His followers answered the call.

On October 22, 2014, a Palestinian terrorist deliberately rammed the car he was driving into a crowd of Israelis standing next to a light-rail train station in Jerusalem. Ten people were injured, and two were killed, including three-month-old Chaya Braun. Innocent civilians were being run down in the streets, the Palestinian leadership was propagating wildly inflammatory statements, and the international community was uninterested. That is, until Prime Minister Netanyahu announced plans to construct over one thousand new housing units in East Jerusalem. The international body immediately leapt into action. The Security Council called for an emergency session to discuss the situation in Jerusalem. Ella came to my office and informed me I had twenty-four hours to prepare a speech. Twenty-four whole hours. They weren't even trying to challenge me anymore.

Together, we drew up a list of everything the speech had to cover: the unbreakable bond between the Jewish people and Jerusalem, the significance of the Temple Mount in Jewish history, the unrelenting anti-Israel incitement on the part of the Palestinian leadership, and the mounting death toll.

Ella surveyed the list and declared, "We need a prop."

Of course we did.

"You know," I started, "they're going to start calling Ron, 'Ambassador Prop-sor.'"

Ignoring my quip, Ella continued, "Seriously. All of Israel will be watching live. We need to make this a good one."

"I'm going to use biblical passages, so he could read directly from a Bible," I offered.

"Yes," Ella immediately agreed, "We're going to need a Bible. A big Bible."

"Right. I think I saw one in Ron's office."

I sent a note to my friend Dan in Rabbi Lord Sacks's office asking for suggestions for a powerful biblical verse to use in the speech and got to work. When I had a draft ready, Ella joined me for our customary line-by-line review. Heads bent over my computer screen, and with the font enlarged to 180 percent because our eyes were strained from weeks of staring at a screen for too many hours, we tinkered and rewrote sections until we were satisfied.

We brought the speech to Ron in his office. As he reviewed, I rummaged through the bookshelves in his office until I found what I was looking for; a large, satisfyingly heavy Bible. Ignoring that it had a prominent El Al medallion embossed on the front cover. I pulled it off the shelf and placed a sticky note by the relevant passages Rabbi Sacks had suggested. Ron finished reading over the speech and gave us his edits. Ella then turned to the most pressing of issues—ensuring the prop was effectively deployed.

"Make sure you hold it up for the Council to see," she instructed. "Do you want to practice?"

"No," came Ron's instant and succinct reply.

No surprise there. We had successfully landed the far more complicated siren-played-off-a-cell-phone prop in the Security Council without ever practicing. Holding up a Bible, even a large and slightly unwieldy one, would be child's play.

Madam President,

"I am here to convey one simple truth. The people of Israel are not occupiers and we are not settlers. Israel is our home and Jerusalem is the eternal capital of our sovereign state.

There are many threats in the Middle East, but the presence of Jewish homes in the Jewish homeland has never been one of them. And yet this is the issue that we have convened to discuss today.

It says a great deal that the international community is outraged when Jews build homes in Jerusalem but doesn't say a word when Jews are murdered for living in Jerusalem. The hypocrisy is appalling.

I have said it before and will say it again. The primary obstacle to peace is not settlements. This is a just a pretext for the Palestinians to avoid making painful compromises. The primary obstacle to peace is the Arab World's refusal to acknowledge that Israel is the nation state of the Jewish people and Jerusalem is the eternal capital of the Jewish people.

. . .

Rather than trying to extinguish the flames of conflict, the Palestinian leadership is adding fuel to the fire. First, they incite violence on the Temple Mount and then they run to the Security Council to complain about the consequences. If this isn't manufacturing a crisis, I don't know what is.

Now let's try to follow the logic. Palestinian extremists have turned the Temple Mount into a battleground by throwing stones and Molotov cocktails at visitors and police. That's phrased as "allegedly" threw stones. We could build a quarry with all the stones that were thrown. In doing so, they are preventing Muslims from praying at their holy site. Israeli police are forced into harm's way to restore quiet and then the Palestinians come to the Security Council complaining about Israel's activities on the Temple Mount.

Do you have trouble following the logic? I certainly do—but I can tell you this, it both starts and ends with the irresponsible actions of the Palestinian leadership.

[EXCERPTS OF EMERGENCY SECURITY COUNCIL SESSION
ON JERUSALEM, OCTOBER 29, 2014]

Thanks to the American delegation, the session concluded with the best outcome Israel could hope for—no resolution and no formal statement condemning Israel. There was no time to celebrate, because hours later terror struck again in Jerusalem. On the evening of October 29, Rabbi Yehuda Glick wrapped up his annual Temple Mount Conference at Jerusalem's Menachem Begin Center. He had spoken to an audience of three hundred people about his efforts to permit Jewish prayer on the Temple Mount. Rabbi Glick walked outside and found himself face-to-face with a man on a motorcycle. The would-be-assassin aimed his pistol at Glick and shot four times.

The Western media covered the attack extensively, albeit in a mulishly-biased fashion. Instead of reporting that Glick advocates for making the Temple Mount a center for religious tolerance where people of any faith can visit and pray, news outlets painted him as a religious radical bent on catalyzing a religious war.

As October turned to November, the terror attacks continued. On November 5, another terrorist used his car to deliberately drive into a crowd of Israelis at a light-rail station. This attack took the lives of Jedan Assad, a Druze police officer, and seventeen-year-old Shalom Aharon Baadani.

On November 9, twenty-year-old Almog Shiloni was stabbed and murdered at Tel Aviv's Hahagana train station. Later in the day, twenty-six-year-old Dalia Lemkus was stabbed to death near the West Bank community of Alon Shvut. This time, the press latched on to the fact that Dalia lived in the settlement of Tekoa, as if this was justification for stabbing an unarmed twenty-six-year-old as she waited for a ride home.

This sort of slanted reporting depicts the mainstream media as lacking any real concern for Israeli lives. The same is true when outlets reject using the term "terrorist" to describe perpetrators of attacks against Israelis. Following every attack, I wrote a letter to the Security Council urging the body to condemn the outbreak of violence. By the end of the week, Ron had had enough. He instructed me to tear up the latest letter and write a new draft admonishing the Council for its indifference to the murder of Jews.

If recent events offer any indication, the Security Council will once again remain silent as Israel buries yet another victim of Palestinian terrorism. Earlier today, a terrorist rammed his vehicle onto two crowded Jerusalem train platforms, killing Jedan Assad and injuring 14 others. Shortly after the attack Hamas claimed responsibility, calling the perpetrator a "martyr" and describing the attack as "a heroic operation." . . .

I write to you today with the full expectation that the Council will continue adhering to its vow of silence. Should the Council revise its policy and deem it appropriate to condemn the Palestinians' leadership's incitement and the violence that follows, I will be the first to commend the Council for embracing sound judgment and upholding international peace and security.

[EXCERPT OF THE LETTER TO THE
SECURITY COUNCIL, NOVEMBER 5, 2014]

At seven o'clock on the morning on November 18, 2014, two terrorists armed with a gun and butcher knives burst into a synagogue in the Har Nof neighborhood of West Jerusalem. Shouting "God is great!" in Arabic, the terrorists rampaged through the small hall. One opened fire at point-blank range on the gathered men, while the second hacked at the victims with a meat cleaver.

The massacre claimed the lives of Moshe Twersky, Aryeh Kopinsky, Kalman Ze'ev Levine, and Avraham Shmuel Goldberg. Eight other worshippers were injured. One of the injured, Chaim Yechiel Rothman, spent almost a year fighting for his life before succumbing to his wounds. The first policeman on the scene, thirty-year-old Israeli-Druze Sergeant Major Zidan Saif, was shot in the head by one of the terrorists and killed. The terrorists, cousins from East Jerusalem, were eventually killed in a shootout with police at the scene of the attack.

As news spread, the streets of Gaza and in the West Bank erupted in celebration. Loudspeakers blared words of praise for the murderers, masked Palestinians posed for pictures holding knifes and axes, and revelers handed out candies.

Every major media outlet covered the Har Nof attack. I'm being generous when I say "covered," because the reports flooding the airwaves and Internet bore little relation to events on the ground. CNN provided a string of appalling headlines beginning with "Deadly Attack on Jerusalem Mosque." After viewers pointed out that the videos and photos being televised were of a synagogue and not a mosque, CNN corrected its headline to read "4 Israelis, 2 Palestinians Killed in Jerusalem." This too drew criticism, so the beleaguered media giant finally landed on "Israeli police shot dead two Palestinian civilians." At this point I stopped watching because I was disturbing my colleagues as I yelled at the screen.

Canada's CBC News ran with "Jerusalem police fatally shoot 2 after apparent synagogue attack." BBC News, my go-to-outlet for skewed Middle

East reporting, didn't fail to satisfy. It headlined "Jerusalem synagogue attack kills four Israelis." Not to be outdone, the equally slanted *Guardian* published a story headlined "Palestinians kill four in Jerusalem synagogue attack," before thinking better—not much better, mind you—and changed it to "Four worshippers killed in attack on Jerusalem synagogue."

It wasn't just the media that had abandoned objectivity. The Jordanian parliament observed a minute's silence in honor of the terrorists. Yes, the terrorists. One MP even demanded the Jordanian government write a letter condemning what he described as "the Zionist attacks on Jerusalem and its inhabitants after a 'heroic act' committed by the two East Jerusalem residents." We had reached the tipping point.

Ron was livid. Between the terror attacks, biased reporting, and one-sided condemnation coming from the international community, he was spoiling for a fight. He had been after me since the summer war to write a speech based on Émile Zola's famous "J'accuse" letter. In 1898, French writer Émile Zola's published an open letter entitled "*J'accuse*" (French: *I accuse*). The letter exposed a military cover-up of evidence exonerating Captain Alfred Dreyfus, a Jewish officer who had been accused of treason by the French army. Evidence of Dreyfus's innocence surfaced following his conviction, but the army hid the information. Zola's letter denounced the military for the cover-up.

Up to our necks in anti-Israeli prejudice at the United Nations, it was time to answer back. We would do so in the upcoming November 29 General Assembly debate.

On November 29, 1947, the UN General Assembly had passed Resolution 181 to establish two states, one Jewish and one Arab. The resolution was adopted by a vote of 33-13, with ten abstentions. The Jews accepted the proposal, but the Arabs denounced the partition plan and promised to defy its implementation by force. Six months later, the declaration of the establishment of the State of Israel was proclaimed, and the following day the surrounding Arab nations responded by launching a war of annihilation. Almost thirty years later, in 1976, the United Nations voted to recognize November 29 as the "International Day of Solidarity with the Palestinian People." Since then, the date has been observed at the United Nations with anti-Israel speeches, films, concerts, and exhibits.

I spent every waking hour working on Israel's November 29 speech, agonizing over every word. I was every bit as fed up as Ron and wanted him to deliver a masterpiece. Whenever he saw me, Ron would pointedly declare, "Klompas, I want to stick it to them with J'accuse!"

In 2014, November 29 fell on a Saturday, so the United Nations scheduled the debate for November 24. I brought the speech to Ron the week beforehand. He had been compiling his own list of ideas, jotting notes on the cue cards he carried in his suit pocket.

Together with Ella, we went through the lengthy list of suggestions. Brimming with righteous anger, he was in no mood for dissenting opinions. We listened in silence and noted every point. By the Friday before the speech, Ron was satisfied with the draft I delivered to him. We had a strong twenty-minute speech ready to go for Monday. I should have known a speech of that profile and significance would be a battle to the finish.

The speech percolated in Ron's head over the weekend. He called me sporadically and, I should add, at hours most humans reserve for sleeping, with his revisions and new ideas. On Sunday morning, Ron dictated a particularly long list of changes. Frowning at my notes, I grabbed my laptop and walked to a local coffee shop to drown my apprehensions in caffeine and got to work. Ron called intermittently with new ideas. It was quite annoying, really.

I wrote and wrote until my eyes were blurry and my nerves were shot from the nonstop infusion of caffeine. Exhausted, I went home and collapsed into bed. On Monday morning, I arrived early in the office and learned Ron had called Ella at midnight with a further list of changes.

"There's a part about Mickey Mouse that you are really not going to like," she warned. Grimly, we made coffee and sat down at my computer. The session in the UN General Assembly was scheduled to start at 3:00 pm and we had a lot of work to do. My father had flown into New York to watch the speech in the General Assembly hall. I had figured the speech would be locked down in the morning and I could meet my dad early in the afternoon to give him a tour of the United Nations, and then escort him to hear Ron's speech.

By noon, I was still at my computer working on the speech. I asked a colleague to meet my dad in the lobby and escort him upstairs through security. He arrived in my office, which was already crowded with Ella and Israel-the-diplomat, who were helping me make changes. I apologized and asked my dad to make himself comfortable in a chair in the corner.

An hour later, Ella and I, with my father in tow, went to Ron's office with a new draft. By now the speech had doubled in length and was a hodgepodge of disparate ideas. Ron read through slowly and we marked sections that could be cut. I hurried back to my office to work on the edits but was interrupted by Dafna calling. Ron wanted to call the ambassador in Washington to get his input. I found an intern and asked her to take my dad on a tour of the United Nations and deliver him to the General Assembly at 3:00 p.m. for the session.

Ella and I hurried to Ron's office where the ambassador was already on the line. I arrived to hear him say the speech was far too long and at least one third had to be cut out. He felt strongly that there had to be a greater focus on Europe, using much stronger language. The ambassador continued to offer his comments, before concluding, "and get rid of that Kumbaya ending."

It was two o'clock, one hour until Ron would deliver his speech, and I could see from the way he was nodding that I would be making every one of the suggestions. I ran back to my computer and began cutting many of the sections that had been added over the weekend and rewrote the introduction and conclusion.

Ella arrived, and we turned to the most sensitive part of the speech about Europe. In recent months, a number of European states had angered Israel by revoking Hamas's designation as a terrorist organization. Next, they pushed for a Security Council resolution to accept an Arab-backed draft resolution to force Israel to accept 1967 borders. The draft, sponsored by Jordan on behalf of the Palestinians, arbitrarily set November 2016 as a deadline for an Israeli withdrawal from war-won lands the Palestinians seek for a state. Several European parliaments had also voted to back the immediate recognition of Palestinian statehood. In October, Sweden went one step further by voting to recognize a Palestinian State. Britain, France, and Ireland followed suit. As it happened, the Swedish minister for state, Annika Söder, would be attending the afternoon session to address the Assembly on behalf of the EU.

Ron wanted to lambaste the Europeans for their misguided actions. As Ella and I batted around ideas, Ron and Israel-the-diplomat appeared at my office door. We had thirty minutes until the session started. Ron calmly sat down beside me holding a steaming cup of tea. He took a leisurely sip and began reading the new sections of the speech.

In the section on Sweden, he said, "I want to use a line about sense, sensitivity, and sensibility."

I thought for a moment and typed, "Nations on the Security Council should have sense, sensitivity, and sensibility. Well, the Swedish Government has shown no sense, no sensitivity, and no sensibility. Just nonsense."

Israel-the-diplomat visibly winced, but Ron nodded, "Good. Add it."

Another joke popped into my head, but I had the presence of mind to keep my mouth shut and not say aloud, "From the country that gave us ABBA, all I can say is Mamma Mia!" The last thing we needed was Ron belting out ABBA's "I've been cheated by you since I don't know when. So I made up my mind, it must come to an end," from the podium of the General Assembly.

Ron continued to survey the section of the speech on Europe and instructed me to reference the Nobel prizes. When I asked why, Israel-the-diplomat explained that Sweden was running for a seat on the Security Council and its support for a Palestinian state was a means of securing Arab support in the United Nations.

The room grew quiet as we all tried to think of a line. An idea came to me and I wrote, "The Swedish Government may host the Nobel Prize ceremony, but there is nothing noble about their cynical political campaign to appease the Arabs in order to get a seat on the Security Council."

I sat back as the others read over my shoulder. It was ten minutes until the session was due to start in the General Assembly. I scrolled to the top of the speech, so Ron could read the new introduction. Ron broke the silence by pointing to a section and instructing me to type what he said word for word, "It is nothing but a hate and bashing festival against Israel."

"Any chance I can say that in a slightly more . . ." I started, but Ron cut me off. "Exactly as I said it."

I had moved the lynchpin *J'accuse* section to the end of the speech, but it still needed a concluding sentence. It was 3 p.m., and the session was starting. I typed out an idea and Ron read aloud as I went. When I was done, he said, "Good," and stood up.

With that, I hit print and called an intern to prepare the copies for the interpreters. We grabbed our suit jackets and UN badges and headed for the car. Ron walked into the General Assembly flanked by me, Ella, and Dafna, just as the introductory speaker concluded his remarks. We strode up the aisle towards the State of Israel's seat and passed the Palestinian ambassador, Riyad Mansour, as he walked toward the podium to deliver his speech. Neither Ron nor Mansour batted an eye at each other.

As we took our seats, I scanned the room and found my father sitting in the wings. When the Palestinian ambassador was done, Ron strode confidently to the podium. He took his place in front of the iconic green marble wall and under the golden emblem of the United Nations. He looked out at the room and began to read his remarks.

Drained, I slumped in my seat, turned to Ella, and said, "That speech almost killed us."

"That was a bad one," she agreed.

When Ron finished delivering remarks, we met him as he descended the dais and exited the Assembly. "What did you think?" he asked.

"It was good," I answered automatically. I was already imaging going home and falling asleep for twenty-four straight hours.

Back in the office, I found Dafna and asked what she thought.

"Darling, you can't tell because you are so caught in the middle of it, but that was the best speech Ron has ever given. That was something special."

"You think so?" I asked skeptically.

"Really, darling."

In the coming days, something strange happened. The Mission's email and phone systems were flooded with emails and phone calls congratulating Ron on his *J'accuse* speech. The speech was spreading like wildfire. It was all over social media, articles were written about it, and the speech was being sent to me with notes saying it was a "must-read."

At events, people would applaud as Ron entered the room and yell, "Hey Ron, J'accuse!"

At one dinner, my table companions learned I was the speechwriter and asked if they could have a photograph with me.

"I can get you a photo with Ron," I offered.

But no, they insisted on a photograph with me.

I was stunned. We had set out to write a powerhouse speech but gotten so lost in the hellish fury of writing it, I didn't realize until days later that we had succeeded. The *Wall Street Journal* printed an excerpt of the speech in its Notable & Quotable section. HonestReporting, a media monitoring non-profit, arranged for the entire speech to be printed as a full-page ad in the *New York Times*. The final triumph came on December 3, 2014, when Congressman Steve Israel stood before the 113th Congress of the United States and said:

Mr. Speaker, I rise today to draw your attention to a speech given last week by Israel's Ambassador to the United Nations, Ron Prosor. Ambassador Prosor spoke passionately before the U.N. General Assembly about the U.N.'s persistent anti-Israel agenda, which continues to manifest itself in many forms such as special sessions, formal inquiries, and one-sided resolutions that single out Israel. I am proud of my steadfast support for the State of Israel and will continue my work to combat the U.N.'s bias against our greatest ally. I found Ambassador Prosor's words enlightening and applaud him for speaking the truth. I would now like to submit Ambassador Prosor's speech.

An excerpt of Ambassador Ron Prosor's address to UNGA on the Question of Palestine, delivered to the UN General Assembly on November 24, 2014, follows.

Mr. President,

As I stand before you today I am reminded of all the years when Jewish people paid for the world's ignorance and indifference in blood. Those days are no more. We will never apologize for being a free and independent people in our sovereign state. And we will never apologize for defending ourselves.

To the nations that continue to allow prejudice to prevail over truth, I say "J'accuse." I accuse you of hypocrisy. I accuse you of duplicity. I accuse you of lending legitimacy to those who seek to destroy our State. I accuse you of speaking about Israel's right of self-defense in theory but denying it in practice. And I accuse you of demanding concessions from Israel but asking nothing of the Palestinians.

In the face of these offenses, the verdict is clear. You are not for peace and you are not for the Palestinian people. You are simply against Israel.

CHAPTER 15

45 shniyot ze kol ma sh'ata tzarich / 45 seconds is all you need

How do you tell them enough is enough?

As we neared the end of 2014, some UN member states were eager to get a jump on their New Year's resolution of finally bringing peace to the Middle East. The Arab Group circulated a Security Council resolution to affirm the "urgent need" to reach a peaceful solution to the situation in the Middle East within twelve months.

What could possibly go wrong?

The resolution was the culmination of three months of hard lobbying on the part of the Palestinians. The resolution read like a laundry list of demands. It set a one-year deadline for the conclusion of negotiations and called for Israel to fully withdraw from all "occupied" Palestinian territories by the end of 2017, and for "a just solution" to all other outstanding issues including Jerusalem, Palestinian refugees, prisoners in Israeli jails, and allocation of water resources. The language grew tougher as negotiations continued, such that a reference to Jerusalem as the "shared capital" of the two states was amended to name Jerusalem as solely the Palestinian capital.

Israel—both the country and the diplomat—strongly objected to the arbitrary and unilateral imposition of terms in place of negotiations and attempted to intervene via backroom negotiations. The United States made it clear that unilateral measures should not predetermine the outcome of diplomatic negotiations. The European Parliament, meanwhile, had already voted to recognize the state of Palestine "in principle."

Much of the criticism leveled at Israel focused on the settlements. There seemed to be an absolute conviction that if Israel would just dismantle its settlements, the conflict with the Palestinians would be solved, which in turn would lead to broad regional stability. World leaders, diplomats, and pundits alike seemed to believe Israel's decisions were just this simple, and the only reason its leaders don't oblige is they are stubbornly misguided. If the conflict were simply about territory—who lived where and built what— it would be one thing. But it's not about territory, it's about two peoples' right to self-definition and self-determination.

According to Peace Now, a left-wing organization that tracks settlement growth, as of 2018, there were 132 Israeli settlements in the West Bank (excluding East Jerusalem) and another 106 outposts, illegally built villages that have not been recognized or authorized by the Israeli government.[*]

About 4 percent of Israeli citizens live in settlement communities that range from a handful of caravans on a hilltop to large and expansive cities with high-rises and tens of thousands of residents. Eighty-five percent of settlers live in blocs near the Green Line (pre-1967 border), covering about eight percent of the West Bank's territory.[†] Given their size and proximity to the Green Line, most believe the blocs will be retained by Israel in any future peace agreement with the Palestinians, in exchange for equivalent land swaps. Other settlements are dotted throughout the West Bank, making creation of a contiguous Palestinian state in the West Bank complicated, if not impossible.

---

[*] http://peacenow.org.il/en/settlements-watch/settlements-data/population
[†] 2018 report from the Israeli Central Bureau of Statistics http://www.cbs.gov.il /reader/shnaton/templ_shnaton_e.html?num_tab=st02_13&CYear=2018

Critics of the settlement enterprise argue they are illegal under international law, citing the Fourth Geneva Convention, which states in Article 49 that, "The Occupying Power shall not deport or transfer parts of its own civilian population into the territory it occupies." In 2012 the Israeli government published the Levy Commission Report, which rejected the applicability of the Fourth Geneva Convention to the West Bank, arguing that area was never a legitimate part of any Arab state. Before 1967 the West Bank and East Jerusalem were under Jordanian occupation, but Jordan renounced its claim to this territory in 1988. The report reads:

Our basic conclusion is that from the point of view of international law, the classical laws of "occupation" as set out in the relevant international conventions cannot be considered applicable to the unique and sui generis historic and legal circumstances of Israel's presence in Judea and Samaria spanning over decades.

In addition, the provisions of the 1949 Fourth Geneva Convention, regarding transfer of populations, cannot be considered applicable, and were never intended to apply to the type of settlement activity carried out by Israel in Judea and Samaria.

*Therefore and according to international law, Israelis have the lawful right to settle in Judea and Samaria, and consequently, the establishment of settlements cannot in and of itself be considered to be illegal.**

Legality aside, I believe that if the Israeli public knew they could secure a durable peace as they did with their Jordanian and Egyptian neighbors, they

---

* https://israelipalestinian.procon.org/sourcefiles/The-Levy-Commission-Report-on-the-Legal-Status-of-Building-in-Judea-and-Samaria.pdf

would agree to concede land for peace. But Israelis don't see a leader with the will and authority to negotiate peace on behalf of the Palestinian people. The Islamist Hamas group controls the Gaza Strip, while the Fatah-dominated Palestinian Authority is the prevailing power in the West Bank. Neither can rightly claim to speak for the Palestinian people as a whole. Hamas, an internationally recognized terrorist organization, is hardly a viable partner. Its 1988 founding document stipulates the goal of wiping Israel off the map. It rejects a two-state solution because, as it interprets Islamic scripture, any land conquered by Muslims at any time in history is a bequest from Allah to the Muslims and can never be surrendered to non-Muslims. In 2017 Hamas released an updated policy platform reinforcing its refusal to recognize Israel and calling for "resistance to occupation, by all means and methods."

That leaves the Palestinian Authority headed by Mahmoud Abbas, a man who is deeply unpopular among his people and has, on at least half a dozen occasions, sought to forge a unity agreement with Hamas. The Palestinian Authority allocates over three hundred million dollars, or about 7 percent of its annual budget, in payments to convicted terrorists and their families. It refuses to pay for the electricity that Israel supplies to Palestinians living in the Gaza Strip, but blood payments to murderers of Israelis are sacrosanct.

In the absence of a trusted peace partner, ceding territory has proven to be perilous. Israel's withdrawal from Southern Lebanon and the Gaza Strip created vacuums that Hezbollah and Hamas respectively seized as launching pads to wage war against Israel.

Israel finds itself in the world's most volatile and dangerous region. Iraq and Syria teeter on the brink of violent chaos. Iran parades missiles adorned with "Death to Israel" through its streets and proudly displays a digital countdown clock to what it says would be the "destruction of Israel." Some news outlets say that the timeframe stems from comments made in 2015 by Iran's supreme leader who said there would be "nothing" left of Israel by the year 2040.* Yemen is on the brink of humanitarian collapse, rivaled only by Syria, where more than half a million people have been killed and millions more have fled to neighboring states that don't have the resources to adequately support them. Lebanon hasn't had a functioning government in years and its dominant political force, Hezbollah, has an arsenal of over a hundred thousand sophisticated rockets and missiles that it uses to threaten Israel.

When it comes to Israel, it's not about borders and it's not about territory. It's about the very character of the Middle East, and whether a region beset by extremism and intolerance can accept the presence of a Jewish democratic state.

———————

But I digress. In late 2014 the Palestinians could not be dissuaded from introducing a resolution to impose terms for a peace agreement, and pushed the Jordanians, who sat on the Security Council, to put the resolution to a vote. In their view, it was a win-win. If the resolution passed, it would be a huge victory, and if the bid failed, the Palestinian Authority would feel justified in seeking membership in the International Criminal Court and pursuing claims against Israel. A diplomatic dance ensued. One day it seemed the resolution would go forward and the next day it was off. As we sat eating lunch together one afternoon, Ella said to me, "You know what? If there is going to be a vote, we should give a one sentence speech."

I paused mid-bite, "What do you mean?"

———————

* Narjas Zatat, "Iranian protesters unveil countdown showing 8,411 days 'to the destruction of Israel'," *Independent,* June 24, 2017. https://www.independent.co.uk /news/world/middle-east/iran-al-quds-day-protest-clock-president-hassan-rouhani -a7806056.html.

Ella continued, "I'm saying we give a one-line speech to show that it's beneath us to take the proposal seriously."

"You want to somehow say that the resolution is so outrageous that we won't dignify it with a response?" I asked. I considered the idea, replying "I'm not sure it will work."

Brushing aside my reservations, Ella continued. "I have two reasons for wanting this," she started. "First, I actually think this is beneath us. And second, Ron is in Israel, so having someone else deliver a one-sentence statement reinforces the message that the Council is wasting everyone's time."

Still unsure, I offered, "Ok. I'll prepare a full-length speech and a second, short 'don't waste our time' version. We'll decide which one to use if we ever get to a vote."

As the days passed, the uncertainty continued. Israel-the-diplomat would call me in the morning and tell me the session would definitely take place the following day, only to call back in the afternoon to say the session was delayed. On Sunday, December 28, Israel-the-diplomat phoned to tell me the vote would absolutely happen Tuesday. By Monday, the session, I was told, was conclusively off.

I left work early and took a walk to enjoy the lights, sounds, and smells of New York in December. The following day things were quiet and I spent the morning tidying my office. Most of my colleagues were on vacation and all of New York seemed to be enjoying the holiday season. In the afternoon, Ella and Israel-the-diplomat appeared at my office door looking grim.

Israel-the-diplomat rolled up his sleeves and said, "The session is happening at five o'clock. We need a speech."

I had already written a speech, so you would think we'd be ready to go. Not so. I had circulated a draft, but nobody had bothered to open the email. I pulled up the file and asked, "Do we know the vote count?"

"We still don't know how Nigeria will vote," Israel-the-diplomat answered.

There are fifteen members of the Security Council, five permanent members and ten temporary members that serve a two-year term. A Security Council resolution needs a two-thirds majority to pass, meaning nine countries would need to vote in favor and all the permanent members would need to withhold their veto.

We knew how fourteen of the fifteen Security Council members would vote. Eight countries would vote in favor, while the United States and Australia would vote against the measure. The United Kingdom, Rwanda, Lithuania, and South Korea would abstain. The final, uncertain vote belonged to Nigeria. If Nigeria supported the resolution, the United States would be forced to use its veto. Washington was working around the clock to either withdraw the proposal or change the vote count to avoid spending political capital on a veto.

Ella came around my desk and pulled up a chair beside me, "I spoke to Ron. He agrees that we should give a short speech."

I pulled up the abbreviated statement I had written. Ella cleared her throat and looked at me expectantly.

"Right," I said and enlarged the text to 150%.

"A little more," she said, shifting closer to the screen.

I zoomed in further and Ella frowned as she read the page of text. "I want the whole thing to be four or five lines maximum."

"Ok. What's the message?" I asked.

"That the Palestinians will try absolutely everything to get a state, except for the one thing they need to do—negotiate." Ella answered.

"Got it," I said and began to type.

It took an hour for us to prepare the four-line statement Israel-the-diplomat would read to the Council. I emailed the lines to Ron and called to get his approval. By the time we got off the phone, it was four thirty and we would need to leave for the Council in fifteen minutes. I turned my attention to another problem. I had expected a quiet day at work and arrived in jeans. Normally, I kept a suit in my office, but it was at the dry cleaners. I considered my options and there weren't any good ones.

"Er, Ella? I don't have any business clothes here."

"Again? You have to be kidding me," Ella said, and surveyed my clothes with a critical eye.

Ella, our polished fashionista, probably had a great many opinions about my generally unkempt appearance, but said, "It doesn't matter. Nobody can see your pants when we're sitting at the table."

She tilted her head to the side and asked, "You have a brush though, right?"

I was rummaging in my bag for my UN pass and a brush when Dafna called, or more accurately, bellowed for me. Dafna is small in stature but equipped with a mighty set of vocal chords.

"I have Ron on the line," she thundered from somewhere down the hall, "Get over here!"

I looked at Ella, "He must be having second thoughts about something."

We trotted over to Dafna's office and huddled around her telephone.

"Hi Ron," I said as I pulled up the speech on Dafna's computer.

"Hi, Aviva-leh," Ron cheerfully replied, "Read me the statement."

I read it out loud and waited. Ron asked me to read it again. He was bothered by one of the sentences and asked for alternative wording. He mulled over the sentence and we watched the minutes tick by. We were going to be late.

I whispered to Dafna, "Text Israel and tell him that we will be bringing an updated statement." Nodding, she picked up her phone and typed furiously while Ella and I spoke with Ron. After much back and forth, we settled the line in question and he gave us the green light. We hung up and I hit print. Huddled around the printer, we watched as it warmed up agonizingly slowly.

When the pages finally emerged, I grabbed them off the printer and ran to the United Nations. Last minute sprints to the UN building were a frequent enough occurrence that I could convince myself they were an acceptable alternative to belonging to a gym. Besides, I didn't have the time, money, energy, or inclination to exercise regularly.

Winded, I arrived at the Security Council and scanned the room for Israel-the-diplomat. I saw him across the room speaking with his American counterpart. I made my way over and apologized for interrupting. The American diplomat gave me up and down elevator eyes, clearly wondering how an out-of-breath, jeans-clad, disheveled lunatic was permitted into the Security Council chamber.

I pulled Israel-the-diplomat aside and heaved, "Ron changed the statement."

"What? Why?" he asked, surprised. I guess he hadn't seen the text from Dafna.

"This is what he approved," I handed him the paper.

Israel-the-diplomat quickly scanned the paper. "Fine."

Just then bells chimed, indicating the Security Council was being called into session.

We took our seats. Israel-the-diplomat sat at the table and I took a seat behind him, self-consciously trying to tuck my legs to the side to hide my jeans.

The session began, and members of the Council took turns delivering remarks. American ambassador Samantha Power described the resolution as "deeply imbalanced," and acknowledged its failure to account for Israel's security needs. She explained, "We voted against this resolution not because we are comfortable with the status quo. We voted against it because . . . peace must come from hard compromises that occur at the negotiating table."

France's ambassador to the United Nations, François Delattre, admitted his government had reservations about elements of the resolution, but would brush aside these concerns, citing "an urgent need to act." The Israeli government was so outraged by France's position that, days later, it summoned France's ambassador to Israel to the Foreign Ministry in Jerusalem. In the meeting, Ambassador Patrick Maisonnave explained France was doing Israel a favor. Yes, a favor! France supported an ill-conceived resolution that threatened Israel's security to *protect* Israel from the off chance of a decades-long legal battle.

———————

The Security Council members finished their remarks and the Palestinian ambassador delivered an address, or more accurately, a diatribe. When he was done, it was our turn. Israel-the-diplomat unhurriedly poured himself a glass of water, turned on his microphone, and then clearly and deliberately read our four-sentence statement:

> *The Palestinians have found every possible opportunity to avoid direct negotiations.*

> *They have engaged in a never-ending string of political games, and now they are parading into this Council with preposterous proposals.*

> *I have news for the Palestinians—you cannot bully your way to a state.*

> *I urge the Council to stop indulging the Palestinians and put an end to their march of folly.*

[STATEMENT TO THE SECURITY COUNCIL, DECEMBER 30, 2014]

It took all of forty-five seconds. Israel-the-diplomat put his paper down, turned off his microphone, and sat back in his chair. The Council members were visibly confused. The ambassadors around the table had settled back into the seats expecting a twenty- to thirty-minute indignant tirade. They looked at Israel-the-diplomat expectantly. Israel-the-diplomat kept his hands folded in front of him and calmly gazed back at the president of the Security Council. The ambassadors turned to one another uncertainly.

The Twitterati were similarly puzzled by our uncharacteristically short remarks. Jonathan Schanzer, a scholar at the Foundation for Defense of Democracies, tweeted: "To give a sense of how few craps the Israelis gave about that vote, they didn't even send their ambassador. And his stand-in spoke for :20."*

After a few moments of hushed whispering, the president of the Council called for a vote. The entire room seemed to lean in and train their eyes on the Nigerian ambassador. When the votes were in, the president of the Security Council noted that eight countries voted in favor of the resolution, two against, and five abstained, including Nigeria. The measure had failed to get the necessary two-thirds majority to pass.

Prime Minister Netanyahu and US Secretary of State John Kerry had phoned Nigerian president Goodluck Jonathan and he had come through for us. We rose from our seats and packed up our papers. I made a beeline for my colleagues and announced, "Let's get a drink."

---

* https://twitter.com/JSchanzer/status/550072323853017088

The next morning, I was scanning the news coverage of the session and came upon a tweet that read: "Official response by @IsraelinUN to Pal. Statehood bid yesterday @UN . . . w/Israeli diplomat in jeans, on her phone."*

Below the tweet was a photo of Israel-the-delegate at the Security Council with me seated behind, clearly clad in jeans and typing intently on my phone.

"What the hell?" I announced to my empty office.

I jumped up and ran next door to Keinan's office.

"Look at this," I exclaimed, showing him the tweet.

Keinan chuckled, "You couldn't even stay off your phone for a twenty-second speech?"

"I wasn't even on my phone while Israel spoke," I sputtered. "I was live tweeting when the *other* delegates were speaking."

Keinan had already lost interest and turned back to his work. I marched over to Israel-the-diplomat's office and showed him the tweet. He threw his head back and laughed and laughed. It is hard to maintain a good fiery indignant outrage when no one will help feed the fury.

That tweet wasn't the only outrage committed that day. Ignoring warnings from the Americans that such a move could lead to congressional sanctions, Palestinian president Abbas signed applications for Palestinian membership in twenty international organizations and treaties, including the International Criminal Court. On top of the military, diplomatic, and media fronts, the Palestinians intended to engage Israel in a lengthy legal battle.

In early January, Ron returned to New York, raring to respond to the Palestinian's Security Council resolution and bid to join the International Criminal Court. He would have plenty of opportunities to speak his mind.

---

* https://twitter.com/SteveMiller202/status/550216781642866688

January brought with it another Situation in the Middle East debate, along with two other Security Council speeches, the annual General Assembly session on Holocaust remembrance, and a special session of the General Assembly to address the global rise in anti-Semitism.

I set to work writing all the remarks, but the forces of HR and IT were conspiring to make my job as difficult as possible. I was supposed to have two interns helping me out, but one had backed out at the last moment. We were waiting for paperwork to come through from Jerusalem to approve the second candidate, but it had snowed in Jerusalem and government offices were closed. Around that same time, an email was sent to all staff instructing us not to drink the water from the taps. If we wanted to use it for boiling water, we were instructed to let it run clear for thirty minutes. It was starting to feel like I was working in a developing country in the heart of Manhattan.

Added to this, the office Internet hadn't been working properly. It functioned at about the speed of dial-up and periodically cut out. For weeks, I'd hear frustrated curses echo in the halls and know the Internet had gone down again. A senior diplomat sent an email to the staff informing us the Internet issues could not be resolved with the current provider and we would be upgrading our lines with a new provider in ninety days. I read his email in disbelief. Ninety days?! How was it ISIS could upload videos from caves in Syria and we didn't have working Internet in the heart of Manhattan?

The printer was also perpetually out of service or spitting out a fine mist of black powder that stained our clothes. I didn't think it could get worse until the maintenance department sent an email informing us that now the water in the taps was brown and we shouldn't even try boiling it. Start-Up Nation, indeed.

On the morning of January 7, 2015, two brothers, Saïd and Chérif Kouachi, forced their way into the Paris offices of the French satirical weekly newspaper *Charlie Hebdo*. Armed with assault rifles and other weapons, they killed eleven people and injured another eleven. As they made their escape, they also murdered a French National Police officer. Within hours, #JeSuisCharlie (French for "I am Charlie") went viral as people declared solidarity for the newspaper's victims and freedom of the press.

Two days later, Amedy Coulibaly stormed a kosher grocery market in Paris, armed with a submachine gun, a rifle, and two pistols. He shot and killed four Jews, Yohan Cohen, Yoav Hattab, Phillipe Barham, and François-Michel Saada.

The other store patrons were taken hostage. Coulibaly ordered them to put down their cellphones, state their name, profession, and origin. The gunman's rant was recorded on a phone that had remained switched on. "They must stop attacking the Islamic State, stop unveiling our women, stop putting our brothers in prison for nothing at all," he raged. After four terrifying hours, French police stormed the store, killed Coulibaly, and rescued fifteen hostages.

The following week, a million and a half people, including more than forty world leaders, gathered in Paris for a national unity rally. Days later, the Security Council held its monthly Middle East debate. With the entire world talking about the tragedies in Paris and the rise of violent Islamist extremism, Ron needed a speech that would resonate.

Mr. President,

I cannot begin without addressing the tragic events that took place in France last week in which radical Islamists launched an attack against our way of life. The slogan of the French Republic is Liberté, Égalité, Fraternité—liberty, equality, and brotherhood. These are the very values that are being attacked.

The terrorists that stormed the Charlie Hebdo office attacked liberty—the right of every person to express him or herself. The terrorist that targeted Jews in a kosher grocery store attacked equality—the idea that every person, no matter his faith, is equal. By aiming their attacks at innocent civilians, the terrorists also attacked brotherhood—the bonds of our shared humanity.

The world responded in force. "Je suis Charlie" and "je suis Juif" became rallying calls to defend our way of life. Millions of people took to the streets of Paris and tens of thousands of people from Boston to Brussels to Buenos Aires rallied to honor the seventeen victims who were murdered. Just as we stood united on the streets, we must remain united in our commitment to uphold freedom.

Make no mistake—freedom is under attack throughout the world. We see it in Nigeria, where innocent people were cut down by gunfire and a ten-year-old girl was strapped into a suicide vest and sent into a crowded market. We see it in Pakistan, where children were gunned down as they sat in their classrooms. We see it in Syria and Iraq, where journalists are savagely murdered. We see it in Saudi Arabia, where a blogger was sentenced to one thousand lashes for running a website promoting free speech. And we see it in Iran, where fifteen people were executed on New Year's Day.

A war is being waged against human dignity and human rights, and we must fight back. Standing united with courage and conviction we can turn back the tide of violent extremism and safeguard the values we cherish."

[EXCERPT OF SITUATION IN THE
MIDDLE EAST SPEECH, JANUARY 12, 2015]

With the January Middle East speech behind us, I turned my attention to the upcoming anti-Semitism event. The informal debate was initiated at the behest of thirty-seven UN delegations seeking to address the rise in violent anti-Semitism worldwide. I sat with Ron to discuss his remarks and he suggested a modern-day twist on the famous passage written by Martin Niemöller, a prominent German pastor and outspoken opponent of the Nazis.

First they came for the Socialists, and I did not speak out—
Because I was not a Socialist.
Then they came for the Trade Unionists, and I did not speak out—
Because I was not a Trade Unionist.
Then they came for the Jews, and I did not speak out—
Because I was not a Jew.
Then they came for me—and there was no one left to speak for me.
[MARTIN NIEMÖLLER]

The morning of the anti-Semitism session, Ron and I were in the UN delegates' lounge waiting to meet Irwin Cotler, Canada's former justice minister and attorney general. We planned to walk over to the General Assembly Hall together with him. I handed Ron a copy of the remarks he had approved the previous evening. Before laying eyes on the page, he let out an impatient sigh.

Oh, how I hated that sigh.

"It's not interesting." Ron lamented. "It's the same blah, blah people always say."

I disagreed but waited. He pulled out his pen and scratched out sections of the speech.

Eye on the paper, he said, "I want a strong sound bite."

"Any ideas?" I asked.

"Something like, we don't need any more monuments to the dead Jews of Europe."

"Oh," I replied, taken aback. "That's quite blunt."

I thought for a moment and offered, "How about we say that we don't need any more monuments for the Jews who were killed in Europe—we need an enduring commitment that Jews can live in Europe?"

"No, no. It has to be stronger. Shove it to them," Ron said testily.

Irwin Cotler arrived just then and was soon drawn into the discussion. I've long been a great fan of Mr. Cotler, but that day I learned he is a diplomat *par excellence.* For thirty minutes, he murmured reassuringly, while tactfully avoided wading into the quagmire. Ella arrived on the scene and we huddled around a computer, eventually settling on this line:

Europe is being tested. We don't need any more monuments commemorating the Jews who were murdered in Europe; we need a strong and enduring commitment to safeguard the Jews living in Europe. If the governments of Europe succeed in defending their Jewish communities, then they will succeed in defending liberty and democracy.

[SPECIAL SESSION ON ANTI-SEMITISM,

JANUARY 22, 2015]

When we were done, we made our way to the General Assembly and took our seats. Several distinguished guests delivered remarks, most notably renowned French intellectual, Bernard-Henri Lévy. American ambassador Samantha Power also took the podium and delivered a particularly stirring speech.

In Judaism, the Sabbath is a holy day of rest and spiritual reflection, when Jews remember the miracle of Genesis and the exodus that followed their ancestors' liberation from slavery. For many Jews, the ritual centers on Shabbat dinner, which begins at sundown on Friday night. Families come together to light the candles and sing the blessings over wine and challah.

January 9, 2015, the day a terrorist attacked a kosher supermarket in Paris, was a Friday. Yoav Hattab, a twenty-one-year-old student from Tunisia, stopped at the market to pick up a bottle of wine to bring to the hosts of his Shabbat dinner. Philippe Braham, age forty-five, went there after dropping off two of his kids at school; his wife, Valerie, had asked him to pick up some food for Shabbat. Yohan Cohen, age twenty-two, worked at the market, and was saving up for his wedding to his fiancée, Sharon. Yoav, Philippe, and Yohan were all in the market when the terrorist walked in. Francois-Michael Saada, a sixty-four-year-old retiree, arrived after the attack started. He reportedly asked to be let in so he could buy loaves of challah.

Yoav, Philippe, Yohan, and Francois-Michael were all killed in the attack. All four were casualties of violent anti-Semitism—targets because they were Jews. All were killed playing some role in preparation for the celebration of Shabbat—a core practice of their faith.

[Excerpt of Ambassador Samantha Power's remarks at a Special Session on Anti-Semitism, January 22, 2015]

Ron listened intently to Ambassador Power's speech. He turned to me tetchily and said, "That's the speech I should be giving."

"Your speech is good," I insisted, but Ron grumpily turned away.

A UN official came to our table to escort Ron to the front of the GA as he was the next speaker. Normally someone from our delegation would sit with him while he waited his turn, but neither Ella nor I made a move to follow.

I whispered to Ella, "Go sit with him."

"No way. You go."

"Forget it," I answered.

A couple of minutes later, Ron rose to the podium and delivered his speech.

Mr. President,

If Martin Niemöller, the German pastor who bravely spoke out against the Nazis, were alive today, I imagine that he would write: "First they attacked the Jews, but I was not a Jew so I did not speak out. Then they attacked freedom of religion, but I was not religious and so I did not speak out. Then they attacked the press, but I wasn't a journalist and so I did not speak out. Then they attacked freedom of speech and expression, but there was no one left to speak for me, because there were no freedoms left."

Mr. President,

Anti-Semitism is a topic that is very close to my heart. My grandmother, Elfrida, was born in Germany and endured the harassment and hardships that a Jew in Europe faced at the time.

By 1936 she knew that there was no future for her or her family in Germany. Just a few months earlier, the Nazis passed the Nuremberg Laws declaring Jews second-class citizens and revoking their political rights. Day by day, she saw Jews being degraded and dehumanized—they were being deprived of their rights, their jobs, and their freedoms. My grandmother took my father and his sister and fled Berlin for Israel.

I was born in Israel thirteen years after the Holocaust ended. Growing up, I knew many Jews who had survived the barbarity of the Nazis. I saw the numbers tattooed on their arms and I heard their heartbreaking stories. In a few weeks, I will become a grandfather for the first time. My son's wife,

Maya, is sitting over there. It pains me to know that my granddaughter
will be born into a world that it still stained by anti-Semitism.”

[Ambassador Prosor's remarks to a
Special Session on Anti-Semitism,
January 22, 2015]

When he was done, diplomats and guests gathered to congratulate him on his poignant remarks. We exited the General Assembly together, and noticeably more jovial, he turned to me and said, "Not bad, Aviva. Let's go to Starbucks."

———————————

A week later, on January 27, Israel's new president, Reuven "Rubi" Rivlin, arrived in New York to deliver a General Assembly speech to mark International Day of Commemoration in Memory of the Victims of the Holocaust. The day of the event, a massive snowstorm shuttered the United Nations and much of New York City. My colleagues worked the phones to reschedule the ceremony for the following morning.

On January 28, Hezbollah terrorists fired anti-tank missiles at an IDF vehicle in northern Israel, killing two Israeli soldiers, Yohai Kalangel and Dor Chaim Nini, and injuring seven others. The attack came after two days of rocket and mortar fire from Syria into Israel. Israeli forces responded and, in the ensuing firefight, Francisco Javier Toledo, a Spanish peacekeeper from the UN Interim Force in Lebanon (UNIFIL) was killed. The situation was tense and had the potential to escalate quickly.

I stood with Ron, Ella, and Dafna at the entrance to the United Nations waiting to greet President Rivlin. We refreshed our phones repeatedly looking for new information. I paced and thought about what to write. At the very least, we would need a letter to the Security Council extending Israel's condolences on the death of the UNIFIL soldier and urging the Council to condemn Hezbollah. I asked Ella what she thought, and she grimly replied, "First we take care of the president, then we deal with the possibility of war."

When President Rivlin arrived, we escorted him to a designated room to meet with the secretary general and president of the General Assembly. Ella and I discussed the letter as we walked over to the nearby General Assembly hall. We were relieved to find the cavernous room filled with delegates and guests who had braved the bad weather.

I took a seat with my colleagues one row in front of the seats reserved for President Rivlin and other VIPs. Israel-the-diplomat found me and told me to get to work on a letter, so it could be circulated as soon as possible. I begged a laptop off a colleague and got to work as the ceremony got under way. From time to time the cameras would zoom in on the VIP row behind us and Ella and I would catch a glimpse of ourselves on the massive screen at the front of the room huddled over the computer.

When the ceremony was over, I jogged back to the office to finalize the letter for delivery. Israel-the-diplomat was feverishly working the phones, urging Security Council members to issue a statement condemning Hezbollah. It shouldn't have been a hard sell given the terror group had already claimed responsibility for killing the two IDF soldiers. The trouble was that the New Year had brought with it new Security Council members, including Venezuela. Anti-American states like Cuba, Venezuela, and even Russia see Israel as a US surrogate in the Middle East and find ways to express their displeasure whenever possible. Venezuela had long been Iran's BFF—that is, its best fanatical friend—and Tehran didn't waste any time exerting its influence alongside other veto-wielding members to shield its patron, Hezbollah, from rebuke.

For an entire week, heated negotiations continued in UN corridors and overseas capitals. The statement that was finally released condemned the killing of a UNIFIL Spanish peacekeeper without mentioning the IDF soldiers who were murdered or the Hezbollah terrorists who were behind the attack. It's hard to conceive of a feebler statement.

> **U.N. Security Council Press Statement on Lebanon**
> *Members of the Security Council condemned in the strongest terms the killing of a UNIFIL Spanish peacekeeper which occurred in the context of fire exchanges along the Blue Line on 28 January 2015. The Members of the Security Council expressed their deepest sympathy to the family of the fallen peacekeeper and to the Government of Spain. The Members of the Security Council looked forward to the immediate completion of UNIFIL's full and comprehensive investigation to determine the facts and circumstances of the incident. [FEBRUARY 4, 2015]*

Ron was incensed and called me at ungodly-hour o'clock and instructed me to write an op-ed about the sordid incident. A couple of days later I brought him an article entitled "Behind the Curtain at the Theater of the Absurd." He chuckled as he read the piece and promptly instructed Anat to pass it along to the *New York Times*. A couple of days later, the *Times* responded by saying they were looking for a "more reasoned and substantive essay."

I made a mental note to use that very same wording in my next letter to the editor. Unfazed by the *Times*'s rejection, Ron instructed Anat to find another outlet to take the article and she promptly handed it to the *Huffington Post*.

Next time I hazard a visit to the United Nations, I will have to check if Hezbollah's flag is flying alongside the 193 nations of the world. In the General Assembly, where nations are seated in alphabetical order, I will venture to see if Hezbollah has been given a coveted blue seat between the delegations of Haiti and Honduras.

And with great trepidation I will scan the halls of the U.N. to see if, in the tradition of all member states, Hezbollah has bequeathed a gift to the U.N. Perhaps it will send one of its Iranian-made Fateh-110 long range missiles—preferably not via air delivery.

Broadway may be down the street, but New York's longest-running tragedy is playing out at the United Nations. At the world's foremost theater of the absurd, the best we can hope for is a limited run."

[EXCERPT FROM "BEHIND THE CURTAIN
AT THE THEATER OF THE ABSURD," PUBLISHED
IN THE *HUFFINGTON POST* ON FEBRUARY 10, 2015]

CHAPTER 16

Sof hammassa /
The end of the journey

What have I learned?

Early in the New Year, I let Ron know it was time for me to move on. His term as ambassador would end in the fall, and I planned to leave around the same time. I could have stayed on under the next ambassador, and it was a tempting prospect because, despite my gripes, I loved representing Israel. But the long days and constant stress couldn't be sustained forever. Added to everything else, the Foreign Ministry workers' strike hadn't led to pay increases for any of the staff, so while my rent and the cost of living in Manhattan crept up, my salary did not. Ron accepted the news and graciously offered that so long as he was ambassador there would always be a place for me on his staff.

Meanwhile, things weren't slowing down in the United Nations. In March, it closed the annual meeting of its Commission on the Status of Women, a global body dedicated to the promotion of gender equality and the empowerment of women, by publishing a report that singled out Israel for condemnation, asserting, "the Israeli occupation remains the major obstacle for

Palestinian women with regard to their advancement, self-reliance and integration in the development of their society."

As in previous years, the Commission had nothing to say about nations that systematically discriminate against women and are complicit in the violence they endure. But then, some of the worst abusers were members of the forty-five-member commission, including Sudan, where girls are subjected to female genital mutilation, and Iran, where women can be punished for crimes of "adultery" by stoning.

The sad truth is Palestinian women face an extraordinary culture of violence, discrimination, and oppression at the hands of their own leadership. Reports from the UN Secretary General have noted that under the Palestinian Authority, there are many barriers preventing Palestinian women from accessing justice and seeking redress. The existing legal framework contains laws that are outdated and discriminate against women, particularly in matters of divorce and child custody. The situation is worse for Palestinians living under Hamas, where spousal rape and honor killings go unchallenged. Instead of shedding light on the challenges facing Palestinian women, the Commission provides cover by blaming Israel.

———————————

That spring, international attention was fixated on the Joint Comprehensive Plan of Action (JCPOA), or Iran deal. For eighteen months, President Obama had made a nuclear agreement with Iran the focus of his foreign policy. He believed that setting strict limits on Tehran's nuclear program in exchange for relief from international sanctions was the best way to prevent the regime from developing a nuclear weapon. Prime Minister Netanyahu and most Israelis believed the Iranian regime had never negotiated in good faith. No matter a deal made on paper, they believed the Iranians would continue developing a nuclear weapon, posing an existential threat to the Jewish state's survival.

In early January 2015, House Speaker John Boehner and Senate Majority Leader Mitch McConnell reached out to Israel's ambassador in Washington to discuss inviting Netanyahu to address a joint session of Congress. A couple of weeks later, Boehner's office informed the Israeli ambassador of their intention to issue the invitation. The speaker's office told the Obama administration of the plan and then issued a formal invitation to Netanyahu. The details of the timing became the subject of considerable scrutiny. The Israeli ambassador knew about the invitation before the White House, but Prime Minister Netanyahu did not formally accept until after the White House had been informed. Many were angered that a foreign government had worked directly with the opposition party, believing it was a major breach of diplomatic protocol. The Democratic Party was outraged at Boehner and the Israeli ambassador for undermining the president and his foreign policy agenda. A fundamental disagreement between Netanyahu and Obama over Iran's nuclear program became a referendum on the US-Israel relationship. Instead of a public debate on the merits of the Iran deal, we got a protracted spectacle of political drama.

The public confrontation between Netanyahu and Obama had been simmering for years. In public, the two leaders spoke about the unwavering bond between the United States and Israel. But the unease was apparent in uncomfortable photo ops, tense body language, and conflicting positions, particularly regarding the settlements, the peace process, and Iran's nuclear program.

This was hardly the first time Israel and the United States had been at odds. There have been disagreements since Israel's earliest days. US Secretary of State George Marshall opposed Israel declaring statehood in 1948. In 1967 the American administration warned Israel it would be alone if it took military action against the Arab world. In 1981 the United States suspended arms transfers for three months after Israel bombed Iraq's Osirak nuclear reactor.

A day before his address to a joint session of Congress, Prime Minister Netanyahu spoke at the American Israel Public Affairs Committee (AIPAC) conference, an annual showcase for the US-Israel relationship. He began by addressing the elephant in the room, telling the assembled crowd, "You see, I'll be speaking in Congress tomorrow. . . . You know, never has so much been written about a speech that has never been given."

He then spoke directly about the issue on everyone's minds: "My speech is not intended to show any disrespect to President Obama or the esteemed office he holds. I have great respect for both." He praised US-Israel security cooperation and intelligence-sharing, before concluding:

> *Ladies and gentlemen, Israel and the United States will continue to stand together because America and Israel are more than friends. We're like a family. We're practically mishpocha.*
>
> *Now, disagreements in the family are always uncomfortable, but we must always remember that we are family.*
>
> *Rooted in a common heritage, upholding common values, sharing a common destiny. And that's the message I came to tell you today. Our alliance is sound. Our friendship is strong. And with your efforts it will get even stronger in the years to come.*

[EXCERPT OF PM NETANYAHU'S
SPEECH TO AIPAC, MARCH 2, 2015]

The following day, Netanyahu addressed a joint meeting of Congress. He was escorted into the chamber by a bipartisan delegation of lawmakers and greeted with thunderous applause. In his remarks, he said,

My friends, for over a year, we've been told that no deal is better than a bad deal. Well, this is a bad deal. It's a very bad deal. We're better off without it.

Now we're being told that the only alternative to this bad deal is war. That's just not true. The alternative to this bad deal is a much better deal.

A better deal that doesn't leave Iran with a vast nuclear infrastructure and such a short break-out time. A better deal that keeps the restrictions on Iran's nuclear program in place until Iran's aggression ends.

[EXCERPT OF ISRAELI PRIME MINISTER NETANYAHU'S
ADDRESS TO A JOINT MEETING OF CONGRESS,
MARCH 3, 2015]

When the speech was done, Netanyahu received a standing ovation from some members, but there was also considerable blowback. More than fifty Democrats skipped the event and House Democratic Leader Nancy Pelosi told the media she had been "near tears" as Netanyahu spoke and accused him of showing "condescension" to the United States. Two hours after Netanyahu left Congress, Obama offered his rebuttal from the Oval Office. He dismissed the Israeli leader's speech as "nothing new" and added that no viable alternative to stop Iran from getting the bomb was offered.

———————

The April Situation in the Middle East debate would be my last. I had grown to both dread and look forward to these speeches and wanted my last one to be memorable. The speech would take place right after the holiday of Passover. In keeping with the tradition of the youngest child asking four questions at the Passover *seder* (dinner), I built the speech around four questions.

Ron gave me a list of topics and ideas he wanted in the speech. He concluded by trying out his latest one-liner on me. He frequently came up with retorts that he could use to ridicule the United Nations' double standard toward Israel, and he wanted the speech to include his latest favorite: "If Jane Austen were writing about the United Nations today, her book could be called *Pride and Prejudice*, but a more fitting title would be Hypocrisy and Double Standard."

Mr. President,

Earlier this month, Jews throughout the world celebrated Passover, which commemorates the liberation of the ancient Jews from enslavement and the birth of the Jewish nation. The seder begins with the youngest child in the family asking four questions known as the "Ma Nish'tana." The child is asking what has changed and why this night is different from all other nights.

. . .

Since our last debate, the chaos in our region has only grown worse. Another nation state has been overrun by radical extremists. First Syria, then Iraq, then Libya, and now Yemen. The extreme elements in our region have displayed a level of barbarism that is shocking even by Middle Eastern standards.

The situation has become so dire that—in a rare display of unity—the Arab leaders have joined forces. It should come as no surprise that they have lashed out with little regard for the consequences. The Saudi-led airstrikes in Yemen have hit humanitarian aid convoys, hospitals, schools, and civilian neighborhoods, and left entire families dead.

And yet there have been zero Human Rights Council condemnations and zero calls for a Commission of Inquiry. If Jane Austen were writing about the United Nations today, her book could be called Pride and Prejudice, but a more fitting title would be Hypocrisy and Double Standard.

On Passover, we ask what has changed. Today, I am here to tell you that unless this Council stops singling out Israel, the only democracy in the Middle East, and starts focusing on the real threats in our region—nothing will ever change.

[SITUATION IN THE MIDDLE EAST DEBATE,
APRIL 21, 2015]

The speech continued with four questions, addressing Iran, Hamas, the Palestinian leadership, and finally—in my own personal parting message to the Security Council—asking what has changed in the international community.

I spent days thinking about the conclusion of the speech and finally decided to connect it to Yom Hazikaron and Yom Ha'atzmaut, Israel's Remembrance Day and Independence Day. I knew I was on the right track when Ella asked me to include a note about Yom Hazikaron in the conclusion and Anat asked me to mention Yom Ha'atzmaut.

I wrote the final paragraphs and concluded by quoting Israel's national anthem, Hatikvah. I sent the speech around to my colleagues for review. The following day Ella sauntered into my office holding the speech. We sat and worked through her edits until we reached the conclusion.

"I love the ending, but we need to take it one step further."

Anat stopped by my office. Ella explained what we were discussing and continued, "I think he should stand as he recites Hatikvah."

Anat could already envision the thundering Israeli headlines and readily agreed.

A few hours later, Israel-the-diplomat came flying into my office, back-pack slung over his shoulder and slightly out of breath, "I don't think Ron should stand," he pronounced, "It's gimmicky and the Security Council isn't the right place for this."

I didn't have a chance to answer before he turned and with a final look over his shoulder yelled, "Tell Ron I don't like it."

Other senior staff also opposed the idea and did their best to convince Ron. The stand or not-stand debate spread through the office with people taking sides and arguing passionately in favor or against. When it came time to read the last lines of the speech, Ron rose to recite the Hebrew words.

Mr. President,

Tomorrow, Israel will commemorate Yom Hazikaron and honor the 23,320 individuals who lost their lives to war and terror. We will remember the brave soldiers who died so that we can have our freedom and mourn the thousands of men, women, and children who were robbed of their lives simply because they were Israeli.

War has never been the choice of the State of Israel. Our choice is and always has been the path of peace. But when war and terror are forced upon us, we will not surrender and we will not back down. For nearly 2,000 years, the Jewish people were stateless and powerless in the face of hatred and indifference. Those days of exile are no more.

On Thursday, Israel will celebrate Yom Ha'atzmaut, our 67th anniversary as a free and independent Jewish state. With great joy and with heads held high, we will celebrate the realization of the words in our national anthem, Hatikvah:

עוד לא אבדה תקוותינו

התקווה בת שנות אלפיים

להיות עם חופשי בארצנו

ארץ ציון וירושלים

Our hope will not be lost,

The hope of two thousand years,

To be a free people in our own land,

The land of Zion and Jerusalem.

Thank you, Mr. President.

[SITUATION IN THE MIDDLE EAST DEBATE,
APRIL 21, 2015]

On top of the Middle East debate, we were gearing up for our annual Israeli Independence Day celebration at the United Nations. The previous year we had impressed our guests by giving them each a SodaStream. It has been Ron's idea to distribute the kitchen gadget that turns plain water into a flavored, carbonated drink. The Israeli company had come under considerable public pressure for operating its factory in the West Bank. Some of the Mission diplomats were certain the guests would refuse the gift, but I didn't see a single ambassador turn it down.

Ron was intent on outdoing ourselves with this year's party. My colleagues on the planning team settled on the idea of showcasing the many flavors of

Israel. Israel is a melting pot of cultures, peoples, and ethnicities. The staff arranged for chefs of different Middle Eastern backgrounds to prepare the food for the event. I loved the theme because the jokes wrote themselves: "A Druze, an Iraqi, and a Libyan come to the United Nations to turn up the heat on Israel. It sounds like the beginning of a joke, but I'm not talking about a Security Council debate, I'm talking about tonight's featured chefs!"

Yom Ha'atzmaut was a rainy and overcast day in New York City, but spirits were high. We arranged to have a shakshuka food truck come to the United Nations and give out free meals to passersby. Huddled under umbrellas, we made our way from the office to the shakshuka truck parked on First Avenue. The Secretary-General had accepted our invitation to open the celebration by being the first to sample the Israeli delicacy. His motorcade arrived, and both the Secretary-General and his wife stepped out. Surrounded by journalists and photographers, they listened to the chefs explain how they made the eggs poached in a sauce of tomatoes, chili peppers, and onions, before accepting a bowl of the steaming dish. The Secretary-General took a bite, looked up, and proclaimed, *"taim meod,"* which is Hebrew for "very tasty." Earlier in the day, his staff had arranged for one of the Israeli security officers working in the United Nations to practice saying this line in Hebrew with him. Ron grinned in delight and responded, "Shakshukah is like Israel—It's a melting pot like our culture, it's hot and spicy like our nature, and once you've tasted it, you always come back for more."

The party moved indoors to a reception room overlooking the East River and one of our former interns was on hand to teach guests Israeli dancing. We watched in delight as diplomats and guests whirled to the Hora. The evening was a huge success and we celebrated after the guests left with a toast or two. Tipsy, we left the UN complex, piled into taxis, and moved the party to a bar on the Upper West Side where we sang and laughed until the early morning.

As my final day of work approached, I grew increasingly nostalgic. I escorted Ron to events and rather than worry about the speeches, tried to soak up the experience. At one event, Ron sat at the front of the room with the VIPs and Dafna and I sat at the back of the room, wine glass in my hand and whiskey glass in hers. Dafna would be leaving the Mission one month after me and was feeling similarly nostalgic. We discussed the amazing places we had been and the people we had gotten to meet. A young singer took the stage and delighted the audience with her exceptional singing voice. When Ron rose to speak, we sat back to listen. The audience laughed and was quickly charmed by Ron's eloquence and funny anecdotes. I turned to Dafna, "We're lucky to work for Ron." She eyed me over her whiskey to see if I was drunk, before nodding in agreement.

Not every audience was as easily captivated. A few days later, I escorted Ron to a lunch at one of the city's largest banks. He delivered a briefing, sprinkling in plenty of his favorite jokes, but the audience stared back impassively. When the speech was over, we stepped into the elevator and Ron asked, "What was with them?"

Shrugging, I answered, "Bankers."

He accepted my answer and announced we would go to Starbucks.

In the car, Ron turned to me and said, "I want one final project from you."

Nervously, I asked, "Oh yeah, what is it?"

"Klompas, you're going to need to concentrate. Really concentrate."

Just then his phone rang. He picked it up, leaned back into the leather seat and began a lengthy conversation. He hung up the phone as we pulled up to Starbucks, "Okay Klompas. Are you listening?"

I nodded. Ron was still fixated on his phone, scrolling through texts.

We walked into Starbucks and gave our orders. As we waited for our drinks, he asked me where he left off.

"Telling me to concentrate," I answered with a smile.

"Yes." He laughed and said, "You will really need to concentrate."

His phone rang. Looking at me seriously, he said, "Stay concentrated." And with that, picked up his phone and began a long conversation.

———

One of our final outings was to an event hosted by then-Congressman Steve Israel. On a warm Sunday, Anat and I met Ron outside his residence and drove to Long Island. The plan was for Ron and the congressman to speak at a private brunch gathering and then attend a community event at a synagogue in Great Neck. We pulled up to a stately home and stepped out of the car. Ron strode confidently into the house and enveloped the host in a warm embrace as we trailed behind. They chatted animatedly for a minute or two, before the host turned to welcome his other guests.

An hour later, we departed the home and climbed back into the car. The plan was for the state police to escort both the congressman and Ron to the synagogue. As we turned out of the driveway, our car horn honked. Curiously, I looked around, but didn't see anything. A minute later, the horn honked again. Oddly, nobody else in the car seemed fazed. After a few more honks I finally asked, "Um, is there any reason why we are honking the horn?" One of the security guards turned to me and said, "It's broken, nothing we can do about it." And so, we drove through the quiet streets of the town, horn sporadically honking, startling people walking their dogs and mowing their lawns. I could see the congressman in the car in front of us turn around and peer curiously through the back window. It seemed like a fitting metaphor for my time working for Israel at the United Nations—loud, curious, and oddly funny.

———

A few days later, I was in my office talking with Jed, who had been hired to take over as the new speechwriter. I was explaining the speech schedule when one of my colleagues came by. I introduced her to Jed. She smiled and said to him, "I hope you'll be patient with me and help me with my writing."

Jed amicably replied, "Of course. I hope you'll be patient with me."

She shot back, "We won't. You're in Israel now."

I laughed. Jed didn't know what he was in for.

As my time at the Israeli Mission drew to an end, I thought back to the day Noa came into my office and asked, "Why would you leave a calm and comfortable government job in Canada to come here and work around the clock for one of the most unpopular countries in the world? Are you crazy?"

Strangely, I would miss the unfiltered advice and candid questions. Turning the question over in my mind, I knew Noa had a point. One did have to be a little crazy to take this job. So, why do it? When so many are so quick to denounce Israel—why take a stand? When Israel is losing support among so many demographics including minority groups, women, and young adults— why speak up? Why commit a career to fighting an uphill battle?

My experience as a member of the Israeli delegation gave me five answers to this question.

Answer one: Israel isn't just a place on a map, it's a map of Jewish history. In Israel, you can walk in the footsteps of Abraham and Sarah and visit the place where Isaac was taken to be sacrificed and Jacob fell asleep and dreamed of angels. You can roam the ruins of King David's palace, see the valley where David battled Goliath, and explore the plains where Samson battled the Philistines. In Israel, the stories of Jonah and the whale, Deborah the judge, and Elijah the prophet come to life. Representing Israel means representing the Jewish people and giving voice to our history and our dreams.

Answer two: Ours isn't just an ancient story, it's an improbable story. For two thousand years, Jewish people lived and died at the mercy of other nations: the ancient Egyptians, Babylonians, Greeks, Romans, the medieval empires of Christianity and Islam, all the way to the Third Reich. That's two thousand years of expulsions, massacres, blood libels, and crusades. A people who have been denied security and autonomy for so long have every right to the security and dignity that comes with having a state of its own. The voice of this nation deserves to speak and be heard in the family of nations.

Answer three: Israel is at the heart of the Jewish people. It is the focal point of countless prayers and dreams across the centuries. Today, half of the world's Jews live in Israel, but no matter where we live, we retain the bonds of family. We mourn as a family and celebrate as a family. We argue like family, give unsolicited advice like family, and fixate on food as a Jewish family is wont to do. Loud and unwieldy, we are united by our history and our connection to Israel. Because whether we choose to live there or not, and whether we choose to visit there or not—we know there is a country in the world that will always open its doors to us. History has made it clear this can never be taken for granted. Being a part of a family means having one another's backs through good times and challenging times.

Answer four: Israel isn't just another state, it's the world's one and only Jewish state. In Israel, the glue on the envelopes and the stamps is kosher. Children dress up as Jewish superheroes like Queen Esther and Judah the Maccabee. The stores sell *hummus* and *haroseth* flavored ice cream. The public buses have signs that encourage courtesy by quoting the Biblical passage, "You shall rise before the aged and show deference to the old." The state's uniquely Jewish character is a distinction to celebrate.

Answer five: Since its first day in existence, Israel has been forced to defend its security from hostile neighbors, its economy from global boycotts, and its legitimacy from international siege. These challenges should make a country callous and closed-minded. But it hasn't. In the middle of the world's most volatile and dangerous region, Israel is a bright spot of freedom and stability and opportunity. I look at Israel and I see a country in which women have presided over each of the executive, legislative, and judicial branches of government; where members of minority groups freely express themselves in the country's boisterous parliament and sit on its independent courts; where a free press openly criticizes government policies; and where every citizen can benefit from the state's open economy. These are lessons for other nations: that a society can preserve its identity without suppressing individuality, and it can sustain its traditions while honoring the traditions of others.

Now, I'm not trying to tell you Israel is perfect. No country is, and I will be the first to say Israel makes mistakes. Like any democracy, there are policies and practices that its citizens and supporters sometimes vehemently disagree with. At the same time, there is no denying that Israel is a self-reflective nation striving to meet the challenges it faces and live up to the dreams of the generations of Jews who prayed for a homeland. Israel is a testament to the ability of a small people to overcome incredible odds by the sheer force of its commitment to knowledge, freedom, and innovation. If the story of the Jewish people and the State of Israel has taught us anything, it's that you don't have to be large to be great. When I would walk into UN Headquarters, I would pass the flags of all 193 member states. There are twenty-five flags with a cross, fifteen with a crescent, and one flag—just one flag—with a Jewish Star of David. We may not have the numbers, but we certainly know how to make an impact.

Ambassador Prosor instructed us time and again to "Walk tall and proud, knowing who you represent and what you represent." This remains some of the best advice I've ever been given. We have every right to walk with heads held high. Israel is one of the freest and most democratic nations in the world, and certainly the freest and most democratic country in the Middle East.

Since 1948 more than one hundred countries have come into existence, and yet not one has won more Nobel Prizes than Israel. In seven decades, its population has grown tenfold and its economy has grown fortyfold. That a tiny and young nation, with few natural resources and persistent conflict, has become a prosperous member of the OECD and a leader in dozens of global industries is nothing short of astounding.

I look at Israel and see a country aspiring to elevate its citizens, its society, and its global contributions. In my eyes, Israel isn't just a country, it's the embodiment of the values I stand for and am proud to give voice to. I could not be prouder to have represented Israel. I have since had jobs where the pay was far better, the hours far shorter, and the colleagues far less mercurial, but nothing has matched the immense pride of waking up every day in service of the State of Israel.